I0120268

Grand Army of the Republic, Dept. of Michigan

Manual of the Grand Army of the Republic

containing its principles and objects together with Memorial Day in the

Department of Michigan, May, 1869 - Vol. 2

Grand Army of the Republic, Dept. of Michigan

Manual of the Grand Army of the Republic
containing its principles and objects together with Memorial Day in the Department of Michigan, May, 1869 - Vol. 2

ISBN/EAN: 9783337221164

Printed in Europe, USA, Canada, Australia, Japan

Cover: Foto ©Andreas Hilbeck / pixelio.de

More available books at **www.hansebooks.com**

MANUAL

OF THE

GRAND ARMY OF THE REPUBLIC,

CONTAINING ITS

PRINCIPLES AND OBJECTS

TOGETHER WITH

MEMORIAL DAY

IN THE

DEPARTMENT OF MICHIGAN, MAY, 1869,

LIST OF OFFICERS, Etc.

EDITED AND COMPILED BY

COMRADE I. M. CRAVATH.

LANSING:

W. S. GEORGE & CO., STEAM BOOK AND JOB PRINTERS:

1869.

"Let laurels, drenched in pure, Parnassian dews,
Reward his memory, dear to every muse,
Who, with a courage of unshaken root,
In honor's field advancing his firm foot,
Plants it upon the line that justice draws,
And will prevail, or perish in her cause."

"They never fail who die
In a great cause; the block may soak their gore;
Their heads may sodden in the sun, their limbs
Be strung to city gates and castle walls;
But still their spirit walks abroad. Though years
Elapse, *and others share as dark a doom*,
They but augment the deep and sweeping thoughts
That overpower all others, and conduct
The world at last to FREEDOM."

CONTENTS.

ADVERTISEMENTS.—Comrade Wm. P. Innis, Real Estate, Grand Rapids; Brisbin & Conely, Druggists; Dan'l W. Buck, Furniture; Pierce & Parmalee, Ruttan's Warming and Ventilating Furnaces; Baker & Ingersoll, Manufacturers; W. S. George & Co., Book and Job Printers; E. B. Millar & Co., Grocers; Jones & Porter, Insurance and Real Estate, Lansing; Comrade Wm. A. Throop, Bookseller and Stationer, Detroit; Field & Leiter, Dry Goods, Chicago, Ills.

THE PRINCIPLES AND OBJECTS

OF THE

GRAND ARMY OF THE REPUBLIC.

———————

The honor of organizing the Grand Army of the Republic belongs to the State of Illinois. The first Post was organized by Col. B. F. Stephenson at Dakota, Illinois, early in the spring of 1866. The Order spread so rapidly that in the July following a meeting was called to organize that State into a Department, at which convention some forty Posts were represented. On the 20th day of November, 1866, a convention met in Indianapolis to organize a National Encampment, at which, Delegates were present from Posts organized in Illinois, Missouri, Kansas, Wisconsin, New York, Pennsylvania, Ohio, Iowa, Kentucky, Indiana, and the District of Columbia. Here was completed, so far as the outline is concerned, our present National Encampment, and the regulations and ritual adopted. General Stephen A. Hurlburt, of Illinois, was chosen Commander-in-Chief; General James B. McKean, of New York, Senior Vice Commander-in-Chief; General Nathan Kimball, of Indiana, Junior Vice Commander-in-Chief, and Colonel B. F. Stephenson, Adjutant General, with headquarters at Springfield, Illinois. From that date the organization continued to grow with unparalleled rapidity, until the entire territory of the United States has been organized into Departments, with the exception of Alaska, and even in that remote region it is expected Posts will soon be established. This astonishing growth, which seems the work of magic, is best exhibited by a tabular statement giving the names of the several Departments, and the dates of their organization, as follows:

Department		Date			Present Commander
Alabama,—Organized	April	9, 1868,—Present Commander, C. Cadle, Jr.			
Arkansas,	"	" 18, 1867,	"	"	—— ——
California,	"	Feb. 20, 1868,	"	"	James Coey.
Colorado,	"	Oct. 20, 1868,	"	"	F. J. Bancroft.
Connecticut,	"	April 11, 1867,	"	"	Theo. G. Ellis.
Delaware,	"	Feb. 1, 1867,	"	"	A. H. Grimshaw.
Florida,	"	Feb. 14, 1868,	"	"	Chas. Mundee.
Georgia,	"	July 6, 1868,	"	"	J. E. Bryant.
Illinois,	"	July 12, 1866,	"	"	Thos. O. Osborn.
Indiana,	"	Nov. 22, 1866,	"	"	R. S. Foster.
Iowa,	"	Sept. 26, 1866,	"	"	J. Williamson.
Kansas,	"	Dec. 7, 1866,	"	"	John A. Martin.
Kentucky,	"	Jan. —, 1867,	"	"	H. K. Milward.
Louisiana,	"	July 8, 1867,	"	"	H. C. Warmouth.
Maine,	"	Jan. 10, 1868,	"	"	George L. Beal.
Maryland,	"	Jan. 8, 1868,	"	"	A. W. Denison.
Massachusetts,	"	May 7, 1867,	"	"	F. A. Osborn.
Michigan,	"	May 6, 1868,	"	"	William Humphrey.
Minnesota,	"	Aug. 14, 1867,	"	"	J. W. Sprague.
Missouri,	"	May 16, 1867,	"	"	R. J. Rombauer.
Montana,	"	Feb. 22, 1868,	"	"	J. H. Mills.
Nebraska,	"	July 10, 1867,	"	"	S. A. Strickland.
N'w Hampshire,"		May —, 1868,	"	"	D. J. Vaughan.
New Jersey,	"	Dec. 29, 1866,	"	"	William Ward.
New Mexico,	"	Feb. 12, 1868,	"	"	H. H. Heath.
New York,	"	April 3, 1867,	"	"	Daniel E. Sickles.
North Carolina,	"	July 11, 1867,	"	"	J. W. Schenck, Jr.
Ohio,	"	Jan. 30, 1867,	"	"	J. Warren Keifer.
Pennsylvania,	"	Jan. 16, 1867,	"	"	O. C. Bosbyshell.
Potomac,	"	Feb. 11, 1869,	"	"	Saml. A. Duncan.
Rhode Island,	"	May 24, 1868,	"	"	Horatio Rogers.
South Carolina,	"	Aug. 28, 1868,	"	"	C. J. Stobbrand.
Tennessee,	"	Aug. —, 1868,	"	"	F. W. Sparling.
Texas,	"	Sept. 22, 1868,	"	"	E. J. Davis.
Vermont,	"	Oct. 23, 1868,	"	"	Geo. P. Foster.
Virginia,	"	Feb. 12, 1868,	"	"	Geo. T. Egbert.
West Virginia,	"	Sept. 12, 1868,	"	"	B. F. Kelly.
Wisconsin,	"	Sept. —, 1866,	"	"	Thos. S. Allen.

This organization began in the Department of Michigan, with the establishment of a Post at Battle Creek, under a charter issued by Gen. Hurlburt, of Illinois, then Grand Commander of the G. A. R.

It is safe to assert that the record of the growth of the Grand Army of the Republic presents a history unparalleled by that of any other organization. Inasmuch as little is generally known regarding the principles and purposes of this organization, it being looked upon by some with feelings of anxiety or jealousy, and by others with sentiments of distrust or hatred, it is proper that we should give a brief statement of its principles and objects, so that the tongue of calumny may be silenced, and the true character of the order may be exhibited to the world. These principles are as follows:

I.—FRATERNITY.

This organization is composed exclusively of those who, in the army and navy and marine corps of the United States, aided in the suppression of the late rebellion. As no nation ever before witnessed such a spontaneous uprising of a great people in defense of their government as took place when rebels sought to sever with the sword the bonds that united these States together, so the peaceful disbanding of the vast army required to protect the nation's life, and their quiet return to the avocations of peace without causing even a ripple of disturbance upon the face of society, was also a marvel to the world. It was but natural that this body of men, for four years associated in the intimate relationship of soldiers in a common cause, should desire to perpetuate the remembrance of the friendships thus formed, the scenes through which they passed together, the hardships and dangers they shared alike, and the glory which is their common inheritance. This is the first great object of this order.

II.—CHARITY.

To seek the good of others, to deal justly, and to love mercy, are traits which rank among the noblest virtues.

Whatever there may be of truth in the proverb: "Republics are ungrateful," it is certain that in times of safety and prosperity men are too apt to forget their obligations to those who, in the hour of danger, risked health and limb and even life itself in their defense. This being the case, it becomes an imperative necessity that the soldiers themselves should see to it that justice is meted out to their comrades in arms—that the crippled soldiers, and those who have come out of the service with health shattered and broken, should be placed under the special care and protection of the government and of society, and that the widows and orphans of deceased soldiers should be cared for, and their necessities supplied. It is plain that such a work can only be done through an organization like ours, which makes the cultivation of this field of duty and of benevolence, its special object.

III.—LOYALTY.

The third principle and object of our organization is to perpetuate the spirit of allegiance to our government; to cherish respect for and fidelity to its Constitution and laws; to frown upon corruption and dishonesty in the administration of our national affairs, and to discourage whatever impairs the permanency of our free institutions, or excites the spirit of insurrection, treason and rebellion among the people of the United States of America. The objects of our order are neither sectarian, partisan, nor political; but fraternal, charitable and patriotic. They appeal only to sentiments that ennoble friendship, commend christianity, and make glorious the love of a people for their country. To affect apprehensions of danger from such an organization, composed solely of the men to whom the nation looked for protection and defense in time of danger, is absurd. Such an organization can be looked upon with feelings of distrust and ill will only by those who saw nothing desirable in the union of these States that it should be preserved; no beauty in the principles of liberty and justice on which our government is based; no glory in the success of our arms.

IV.—Remembrance of the Fallen.

Had the Grand Army of the Republic no other object, the commemoration of the services of our Memorial Day is one worthy to command the sympathy of every true American heart, and the coöperation of every true soldier of the Republic. It is a sufficient honor that this Order inaugurated this National Anniversary, and that to them is entrusted its observance. Let us, as our ranks become thinner from year to year, close up around the graves of our fallen comrades, till our rear guard crosses over to where—

> " On fame's eternal camping ground
> Their silent tents are spread,
> And glory guards with ceaseless round
> The bivouac of the dead."

V.—The Grand Army's Bequest.

This is a feature not yet adopted, but that something like the plan proposed at the recent National Encampment, and which is embodied in this work, will, with some essential modifications, be engrafted into the organization there is no doubt. It will be noticed that one feature of this scheme, as presented, contemplates that only those who have become members of the Grand Army of the Republic prior to January 1st, 1871, will be entitled to avail themselves of its benefits.

EXTRACT FROM THE WELCOMING ADDRESS OF GEN. W. H. BALDWIN, TO THE NATIONAL ENCAMPMENT OF THE G. A. R., HELD AT CINCINNATI, OHIO, MAY 12 AND 13, 1869:

" Since the close of the war, in which those ties of friendship were formed which it is one of the objects of this organization to strengthen and perpetuate, you have been engaged in the pious duty of relieving the sufferings of your afflicted comrades, and administering to the wants of their destitute families. These soldiers, who were disabled in the country's service, receive at your hands sustenance, and sympathy, and watchful care while they linger with us, and when their sufferings are ended, it is from you that they receive a decent burial. The aged widow, whose sons fell in battle, in her poverty, and friendliness, and desolation, looks to your benevolent Order for assistance. The destitute orphans of your comrades, who gave their lives to the country, are the special objects of your care. The State owes them a debt not to be canceled by thrusting them into poor-houses and prisons. It has been largely through your exertions in their behalf that in several of the States homes have been established for the orphans of deceased soldiers, where the children of your dead comrades may be cared for and properly educated, that they may grow up worthy and respectable citizens. It is proper, it is natural, that soldiers should care for their deceased comrades, and for the widows and orphans and mothers of those who have lost their lives fighting valiantly side by side with them. But there are other reasons than those of benevolence and charity which make the acts of your Order matters of solicitude to the far-seeing statesman and thoughtful citizen. In a Republic, relying upon her citizen soldiery, it is a matter of the highest importance that patriotism and heroic deeds should be appreciated and properly acknowledged; that the memory of the dead should be honored, and that the families of those killed in battle should be distinguished from the victims of thriftlessness and vice. The nation that honors and rewards her defenders; that cherishes the memory of her heroic dead, and makes the orphans of those who die for the country the wards of the State, will never call in vain for volunteers to suppress rebellion, or to repel invasion. The man upon whom no helpless one leans for support, can smile in the face of death. For him to be brave is small merit—it costs him little; but for the father of helpless children, whom he could rear in comfort and luxury, but who, by his loss, would be deprived of their only support, for him to meet death with composure, requires more than Roman fortitude.

As the heart-rending history of the orphans of soldiers once in good circumstances has come to my knowledge, I have thought that the prospect of leaving one's little children to such a fate, might well make cowards of the bravest. Let us hope that our efforts in behalf of the orphans may be crowned with success.

In addition to your care for the living, you have gathered the remains of many of your fallen comrades and placed them in cemeteries, where their last resting place is protected from sacrilegious intrusion. The General Government is doing much in the same direction, and at no very distant day it is believed that the remains of all those soldiers whose burial places are known, will be properly cared for.

You have inaugurated the beautiful custom in the spring-time of the year, of performing the sacred rite of decorating with flowers the graves of your fallen comrades. This is a custom which we trust will live after the present generation of soldiers shall have passed away. But it is with sadness that we remember the many thousand soldiers who rest in unknown graves, or who lie unburied, never having received the rite of sepulture. No stone marks their last resting place, and no friendly hand will strew flowers over their sacred dust. But their virtues are remembered, and their memories cherished by their surviving comrades.

> " By fairy hands their knell is rung ;
> By forms unseen their dirge is sung ;
> There Honor comes, a pilgrim gray,
> To bless the turf that wraps their clay ;
> And freedom shall awhile repair,
> To dwell a weeping hermit there."

ADDRESS OF GEN. JOHN A. LOGAN, DELIVERED AT CINCINNATI, OHIO, MAY 12, 1869, AT THE OPENING OF THE NATIONAL ENCAMPMENT OF THE G. A. R.

COMRADES:—Within the past few years, history has been enriched with two events so manly in their inception, and so sublime in their results, that they may well be called the leading facts of the age, alike creditable to our nation and mankind.

First. A vast, well organized army, recruited from a brave and hardy population of twelve million souls, making war against our government, well supplied with all necessary appliances, and enjoying the aid and sympathy of powerful allies, has been utterly crushed.

Second. The conquerors of this stupendous power have retired to civil life, and been absorbed in the great mass that embodies our industrial activities, without suffering, without disorder to the commonwealth, and without producing a plethora of labor.

Our great war, comrades, with its innumerable scenes and incidents, its trials, toils, sufferings and triumphs, has been the theme of frequent and elaborate song and story, but the sublime tranquility that followed the disbandment of our armies remains, comparatively, a field untrodden.

Let us contemplate the position of affairs in the memorable month of April, 1865.

The rebellion was ended. A fugitive traitor President was hiding among the pines of Georgia. The vast hordes that withstood our blows during four years of belligerent action were scattered to the winds. Our armies, embodying more than a million men, inured to conflict that usually excites and stimulates the worst passions of our natures, having no more foes to combat, who could say that they would not repeat the history of olden times, and wage war among themselves or upon their friends?

Under these circumstances, the order was given—"Break up these armies." Such soldiers as have homes must return to them, and such as have none must seek them among their countrymen.

In classic days, both republican and imperial Rome had been shaken to its centre by disbanded soldiery, while in Greece and Spain the mountain fastnesses had been filled with desperadoes from such bodies, whose subsistence was wrung from passing travelers or peaceful haciendas. Even our neighboring Republic of Mexico had furnished examples of the danger to mankind of forcing bodies of soldiers from their avocation to the quiet scenes of ordinary life.

But neither Rome, Greece, Spain, nor Mexico, was ever tried by such an ordeal as ours. Their disbanded armies were, in comparison with ours, almost as nothing. In fact, there is not in human history a case cited, except ours, in which a million of soldiers were, in a day, removed from belligerent to peaceful life. Probably there is no government on earth, except our own, that would have dared to try the experiment. I am confident there is no other in which such trial would be safe.

But we were disbanded. Departments, corps, divisions, brigades, regiments and companies, almost within the hour, disappeared like the morning mist. We had appeared upon the field at our country's call, as promptly as the clansmen of Roderick Dhu burst into view upon their Alpine hills, and as soldiers we passed away almost as readily, at the waving of a hand.

Was there no ambitious leader dissatisfied with the distribution of war-like laurels, ready to gather the scattered host, seize the power and archives of the nation, and make himself a king? Were there no fastnesses among our mountains in which brigands might find concealment, and carry on a war of depradation on mankind? Perhaps there were such rebellious spirits, but the soldiers themselves, the mass of the disbanded host, were beyond the power of seduction. They loved the government for which they bled, the flag under which they had marched to victory, and would prefer to die in defense of liberty, rather than live in opulence upon its ruins.

No outbreak, no revolution, no disaster of any magnitude has followed the segregation of these million warriors. They sought their homes with joyful hearts and tuneful voices. There were no tears of mourning over the cast-off trappings and habiliments of strife. The hand grown cunning in the use of arms applied itself to the axe, the hammer, the loom, and spade. Battle shouts had given place to exultations over victory, and these, in turn, were followed by the songs of joy, of love, and peace, that sanctify that place of Heaven called home.

Very much of this sublime result is due, doubtless, to the form of government under which we live. Much is attributable to the educational influences among which we were reared, and much, very much, to the organization known as the "Grand Army of the Republic."

This Order originated in a desire for mutual protection, aid, and education. We never feared that the toils and sufferings of our soldiery would be forgotten, or fail to be appreciated by the mass of our countrymen, but we did fear that high officials might at times be prompted by their selfishness to disregard or neglect us.

Politically, our object is not to mingle in the strifes of parties, but by our strength and numbers to be able to exact from all a recognition of our rights with others.

We desire further by this organization to commemorate the gallantry and sufferings of our comrades, give aid to bereaved families, cultivate fraternal sympathy among ourselves, find employment for the idle, and generally, by our acts and precepts, to give the world a practical example of unselfish, manly coöperation.

Thus far our efforts have proved successful. The report of the Adjutant General will present fully the history and progress of our Order, and more than sustain our highest hopes of the future. The burden of many crosses has been lifted from many hearts. Famishing souls and bodies have been fed. Manly excellence has been developed and cultivated, while public, social, and domestic life among our comrades has been purified and blessed through our humane endeavors.

I congratulate you, comrades, that we have now a national administration which is not unmindful of the soldier. He is filling important places of trust and profit. He is welcomed at the Presidential Mansion. Along the street a crutch or empty sleeve insures respect, and in the public convocation he receives attention and applause.

I congratulate you, also, that our Order flourishes now as it never has done before, and that peace, tranquility, and industry are comparatively universal among ourselves and throughout our national domain.

Let us foster and cherish this benevolent Order, so useful in the past, so beneficent in the present, and giving such promise for the future. Let us unite in vigorous efforts to extend and perpetuate its power.

While in the flush and strength of manhood, we may not fully grasp and realize the fact that man's true interest lies in doing good; but when the golden bowl of life is breaking; when our faces become carved in storied hieroglyphics by the stylus and pantagraph of age, each act of kindness done, each word of kindness spoken, will, by natural compensating law, return like the dove of Ararat, to the soul from which it was sent, and bearing with it branches of unfading green from the Post "beyond the river."

RESOLUTIONS ADOPTED BY THE NATIONAL ENCAMPMENT, G. A. R., MAY 13, 1869.

Whereas, The organization known as the Grand Army of the Republic, is founded upon the glorious and world-wide embracing principles of fraternity, charity, and loyalty to our flag and country;

And whereas, Its success in the past is the best guarantee of its future prosperity;

And whereas, The welfare of our living comrades, and that of the orphans and widows of the honored dead, and the maintenance of our sacred principles, demand renewed efforts in its behalf; therefore, by the National Encampment, through the representatives here assembled, be it

Resolved, That the destiny of the Grand Army of the Republic is not fulfilled, until it shall embrace within its protective folds, every one of the million of honorably discharged soldiers of the several armies of the service during the late war of the rebellion; until the families of those requiring assistance are beyond the reach of want, and their children properly educated and cared for by the country; and until the last faithful veteran soldier has surrendered without dishonor to the Great Conqueror of all mankind, and has been released from his bonds, and mustered into a grander army above.

Resolved, That it is through this organization alone that the bonds of fraternal feeling can be successfully sustained and strengthened, and the electric currents of sympathy and brotherly affection, born of common toil and danger, be evolved and hastened in their courses through the thousand hearts scattered over the wide expanse of our ever-growing empire.

Resolved, That that charity which speaks through kind actions and benevolent deeds, and sacrificing efforts for those associated with us, shall ever be one of our cardinal principles, and carefully exemplified in our practice.

Resolved, That we shall cling to the principles and practices of loyalty to our flag and country, with the same pertinacity and energy with which we sustained it in the field; and that no foe, foreign or domestic, shall ever find us backward in rushing to the rescue of the Government we have saved, by whatever danger it may be assailed; that our hearts still beat time to the "music of the Union," and will ever be found vibrating in harmony with the pulsations of the national life.

Resolved, That whatsoever suspicion of political nature may have heretofore attached to the Grand Army of the Republic as to its being a political organization, that we hereby declare it above, and independent of all partisan feeling and action, and actuated only by a determination to sustain to the fullest extent, the principles so clearly defined in the rules and regulations adopted by the National Encampment, and embracing only the patriotic duties enjoined by charity, fraternity, and loyalty to flag and country, including a just condemnation of that fell spirit of rebellion, which would have destroyed not only the country, but rooted liberty itself out of the land.

Resolved, That in the name of our comrades scattered throughout this broad land, we desire to express our gratitude to the citizens and legislators of those States, which have established homes and schools for the maintenance and education of the orphans of our deceased brethren, and that we invoke the blessings of Heaven upon them. And that we earnestly urge upon the citizens and legislators of those States where no such provision has been made, to take immediate steps to fulfill the obligations imposed upon them by the casualties of the late war, and to redeem their pledges made to the brave volunteers, to care for their families during their absence, and in case of their death, by establishing homes for both orphans and widows, so far as their necessities may demand.

Resolved, That the pledges and recommendations made by conventions and legislative bodies to give preference to soldiers (other things being equal) for appointment to civil avocations and government positions, whereby our disabled comrades might serve both the country and themselves at the same time, and be enabled to earn an honest and honorable livelihood, are daily impressed upon our minds by the fact that their claims for labor and positions are, in many portions of our country, almost entirely ignored; and that, in the name of our crippled comrades, we respectfully ask the honorable redemption of those pledges.

"THE GRAND ARMY'S BEQUEST."

A Plan of Mutual Life Insurance for all Members of the Grand Army of the Republic.

Respectfully suggested by E. F. M. Faehtz, Assistant Quartermaster General, Department of the Potomac, G. A. R.

The Grand Army's Bequest is to be organized under the laws of the United States as a coöperative association, for the benefit of the heirs of the deceased comrades of the Grand Army of the Republic, and will be chartered by Congress as a national incorporation.

I. *Object.*—The object of the corporation is to provide and secure a certain sum of money, not less than one thousand dollars, to the heirs of each deceased member.

II. *Admission to Membership.*—The conditions of admission to membership in the corporation are, that an applicant must be a comrade of one of the Posts of the Grand Army of the Republic, of good standing; that he must accompany his application by fifty cents admission fee; and that the application must be filed before the first day of January, 1871. After this date the number of members cannot be increased under any condition.

No restrictions whatever are made as to age, condition, habits, state of health, or anything else in regard to the qualification of an applicant.

III. *Forfeiture of Membership.*—Non-payment of dues for more than five consecutive cases, and voluntary surrender or transfer of a certificate of membership to another member, will terminate the same; but there are such provisions in the by-laws of the corporation as to protect any member, or his heirs, against loss of the benefits in cases of involuntary dereliction or excusable neglect.

No cause or manner of death, nor geographical limitation, shall deprive the heirs of a deceased member of the benefits of the corporation.

IV. *Rights and Duties of Members.*—Each member has a right of holding as many certificates of membership, not exceeding ten, in his own name, as the number of times he pays the admission fee of fifty cents, for each time of which he receives a certificate of membership in book form.

Each member has also the right of acquiring certificates of other members in a legal transaction, and with the knowledge of the officers of the corporation, or the right of transferring his own in the same manner.

The duties of members consist in the payment of dues, amounting to one cent for each certificate in each case of death of any member of the corporation, until such payments are discontinued, as provided in paragraph 7, and in a general compliance with the by-laws of the corporation.

V. *Organization.*—As working organization of the corporation, the present structure of the Grand Army of the Republic is adopted for all purposes of correspondence and collection of dues, with perfect equality of rights and duties of all members. These members shall, according to geographical demands or their own preference, belong to a branch association, called, under the present Rules and Regulations of the G. A. R., *Post,* and a number of these Posts, as at present, form what is called *Department.*

Individual members transact business with their Posts, these with their Department, and the Departments with the *Central Bureau* of the corporation in all cases but those directly bearing upon the disbursement of the benefits in a case of death, when the heirs or claimants forward their proofs of claim and death, as prescribed in the by-laws, directly to the Central Bureau, and receive the amounts due them directly from the same. Such payments are made in all uncontested cases, within sixty days from the date of the notification of the death of a member.

VI. *Financial Administration.*—The financial administration of all collective funds of the corporation is vested in the Central Bureau, consisting of—

1. A Board of Trustees, annually to be elected in the regular meeting of the National Encampment of the Grand Army of the Republic.

2. A corps of paid employés, to be appointed by the Board of Trustees, from among such as are recommended by the National Encampment. The rights and duties of the Trustees, as well as the employés of the Central Bureau, shall be defined in the by-laws of this corporation.

VII. *Resources.*—The resources of this corporation shall consist in all funds accruing from the payments of admission fees, dues of members, and of the interest from the investments of the same. The payment of dues is discontinued after the first half of the total number of members have died, because, by this time, the reserve fund of the corporation has accumulated more than sufficiently to pay the claims of the heirs of all the then surviving members, and the further payment of dues would be an unnecessary and grievous tax on the survivors.

VIII. *Disposal of the Resources.*—The sums accruing from these resources shall be disposed of in the following manner :

1. The amount accruing from the admission fees shall be used under the direction and orders of the Board of Trustees, to defray the necessary expenses of the Central Bureau during the first year. Any surplus over and above these expenses shall be invested in the manner as specified in paragraph 10.

2. The amounts accruing from dues shall be divided as follows :

(*a.*) As many cents as half the number of members at the beginning of this organization, or, in other words, half as many dollars as there are hundreds of members on the first day of January, 1871, shall be paid without deduction, to the heirs of each deceased member.

(*b.*) The entire balance of the amounts of dues accruing in each case of death shall be invested in U. S. bonds, and form a reserve fund for the payment of the claims of the heirs of such members as survive the first half of the total number of membership.

The *interest* accruing from all investments for the reserve fund, shall be disposed of in the following manner :

(*a.*) The expenditures of the Central Bureau, as well as all necessary expenses of printing, advertising official statements, stamps, and other incidentals, shall be paid upon the order of the Board of Trustees.

(*b.*) A part of the remaining sums of interest, after the payment of the specified expenditures, may be, upon the recommendation of the National Encampment of the Grand Army of the Republic, but only with the approval of the Board of Trustees, appropriated for the purchase and permanent improvement of real estate, which may be rented for the uses and purposes of the G. A. R., but sufficient guarantees must be given to the Board of Trustees that such investments would not yield less income than the amount thus invested would yield interest when invested in United States bonds ; and that no loss, either in value or revenue, would arise from such investment to the assets of this corporation. Also, the part so appropriated shall never exceed one-half of the remaining interest.

(*c.*) All sums not provided for in the foregoing stipulations shall be invested in the manner prescribed in paragraph 10 for the investment of the Reserve Fund, and shall form part of the same.

IX. *Provisions for Expenditures.*—The expenditures of the Central Bureau, as well as the incidentals specified above, and others, shall be regulated and superintended by the Board of Trustees, with as much economy as the dignity and prosperity of the corporation will demand. As already stated, they shall be defrayed for the first year out of the funds accruing from the admission fees, and for the following years out of the interest emanating from the investments of the Reserve Fund. Extraordinary expenses, as p. c. legal advice and others, must be provided for by the Board of Trustees, from the resources of the Reserve Fund of the current year in which they occur.

X. *Investment of the Reserve Fund.*—All moneys accruing from any source whatever, for the Reserve Fund, shall be, by the direction of the Board of Trustees, invested in United States bonds, or, under very safe and favorable circumstances, in real estate.

Speculations of whatever description with funds of this corporation are, without exception, strictly prohibited.

Receipts of interest in gold are to be utilized at the market value, within forty-eight hours after the first meeting of the Board of Trustees subsequent to the date of receipt.

XI. *Dissolution of the Corporation.*—As the number of members, after the 1st day of January, 1871, cannot be increased, no new members can be admitted, and by the law of nature must grow steadily smaller, and finally expire, therefore the following provisions are made for the final dissolution of the corporation and the disposal of its estate :

Whenever the number of members grows less than 50,000 (fifty thousand,) the Board of Trustees shall officially notify the President of the United States of such fact, and respectfully request him to appoint, with the approval of the United States Senate, a committee of 3 (three) gentlemen, the salary of each of whom shall be $5,000 (five thousand dollars) per annum, payable out of the revenues of this corporation. The members of this committee, who, if possible, ought to be members of this corporation, shall meet and enter upon their duties upon the first Monday of July following their qualification, in the city where the Central Bureau of this corporation is located, to receive from the Board of Trustees an exact official statement of all the assets of this corporation over and above the amount necessary to satisfy the claims of the heirs of the still surviving members. This statement is to be repeated on the first Monday of each following month, when the committee will meet, until the number of members is less than one thousand, (1,000,) when the Board of Trustees shall surrender their trust into the hands of said committee on the first Monday of July subsequently.

This committee then enters into all the rights and duties of the Board of Trustees until the last member of the corporation has died, when they shall discontinue the Central Bureau and turn over all the funds and assets of the extinct corporation into the hands of the United States Treasurer, who shall at once, in the presence of the committee and the Secretary of the Treasury, cancel and destroy all United States bonds and coupons then in possession of the estate of the extinct corporation, and shall cause all property belonging to the said estate to be sold by public auction, and the proceeds thereof, as well as all other funds belonging to the estate, be used to pay, as far as they reach, any portion of the national debt which may be unpaid at that time, and if such portion should not exist—that is to say, if the entire national debt should be redeemed—the entire estate to be divided into two equal parts. The first one of these parts shall be devoted and expended for the erection of a monument in the city of Washington, to the memory of the defenders of the nation in the late rebellion, and the other half shall be dedicated to educational purposes, under the direction of the United States Congress.

THIS IS THE GRAND ARMY'S BEQUEST.

XII. *Illustration of the Working.*—From the foregoing provisions it will be manifest that the Central Bureau of the corporation corresponds with what insurance men call the "Head Office,"—the National Encampment of the G. A. R. with "meetings of stockholders by proxy;" the Departments with "agencies," and the Posts with "sub-agencies," with the difference that the mechanism is much more simple and economical, as there are no salaried officers, except in the Central Bureau, and no advertisements and other expenses for solicitations or other services rendered.

On the first day of March, 1869, the official returns of the G. A. R. showed thirty-seven Departments, with an aggregate of 240,000 members, which number, however, has already, and will be before January 1, 1871, much increased by accession of new members, as well as by the taking out of more than one certificate of membership by individual members. Taking, however, the basis of only 200,000 members for calculation, we find that the admission fee for this number will amount to $100,000,—a sum certainly more than sufficient for the establishing and working of the Central Bureau for the first year.

The dues in the first case of death will amount to $2,000, of which, after payment of $1,000 to the heirs, the other $1,000 are invested for the Reserve Fund.

As the Grand Army consists only of comrades who have served during the late war, it is evident that nearly all of them are of an age between twenty-five and sixty years, and although in some cases invalids and cripples, the large majority of them are what insurance men would call " good risks."*

Taking, then, from the average mortality tables, the very highest figure of 12.5 deaths in 1,000 per annum,† the first year of the corporation's operations, ½-cent dues only, would call for 2,500 deaths, and would account for a receipt of dues of $2,500,000, less an outfall of $32,250, which is taken in consideration in the subsequent calculation. One million two hundred and fifty thousand dollars would be paid to the heirs, and the balance would go into the Reserve Fund.

We now assume forty years as the time necessary or probable for the mortality of 100,000 members, and find that not even counting the considerable amounts accruing from immediate investment of payment during fractions of the year, the Reserve Fund will amount to at least $193,452,-457. Allowing now the large amount of $45,000 per annum for expenditures, and calculating it with compound interest for forty years, which amounts to $6,964,288 47,—add to this the amount accruing from the fall-out in dues, $50,005,000, we have $56,969,288 47, and reserve for the heirs of the survivors $100,000,000, and deduct this total of $156,969,-288 47, and we find still a surplus of $36,483,169 53 in the Reserve Fund ; but this amount will be much higher in reality, as we have, for the safety of the calculations, made great allowances.

Such a result speaks for itself; not only that the heirs of all the members would be provided for as handsomely as the deceased member had desired, but the corporation, after its termination, would leave to the nation the respectable amount of not less than fifty millions of dollars.

---

* This view is strongly corroborated by the late statistics of the veterans of the first French Empire, (vide April, 1869,) showing, fifty-four years after the close of the Napoleonic wars, forty thousand survivors.

† A very reasonable assumption; but even if incorrect, would not change the results of the calculation, as the resources increase with the mortality greatly, while it only very little increases the individual tax.

XIII. *Advantages.*—These glorious results of the scheme being shown, there need be little said as to its advantages. The corporation, if the Trustees do their duty, cannot but be in the most prosperous condition during its existence, and losses are an impossibility under proper management.

The individual members have the comfort for a very small payment, which otherwise hardly could be utilized, to secure to their dear ones a handsome provision after their death.

For one cent on each death, or an average annual payment of $25, they secure at least $1,000 to their heirs. For two cents, or $50 per year, $2,000. For five cents, or $125 per annum, $5,000.

There is no insurance company in the world which could equal or even approach such results.

In every case, even the very last of death, the heirs receive at least as much as has ever been paid in, and in not less than 100,000 cases they receive much more than the accumulated payments would amount to.

All conditions are equally just and lucrative to the poor as to the wealthy.

No invalid or sufferer is excluded for his misfortune.

No act of a member, except the willful discontinuance of membership, can deprive his heirs of the benefits of this corporation.

And last, but not least, after all have been provided for, the members leave a munificent token of love to the nation, which they have loved so well during life.

REMARKS.

The above plan was presented, as will be seen, at the National Encampment, May 13, 1869, and a committee appointed to thoroughly investigate the practicability of the scheme, in accordance with the following resolution adopted by the Encampment:

Resolved, That a committee of five be appointed by the Chair, to examine into the practicability of connecting a scheme of coöperative life insurance, with the Grand Army of the Republic. This committee shall be empowered to correspond with acknowledged authorities upon the subject of life insurance, and it shall be their duty to take all steps advisable to elucidate the merits and demerits of any submitted or proposed plan. It shall also be their duty to report, at least four months before the next meeting of the National Encampment, the final results of their labors, to the Commander-in-Chief of the G. A. R., who will communicate the same to the Departments, that they may thoroughly discuss the subject, and be prepared to instruct their delegates in the next National Encampment, what action to take in the premises.

The Commander-in-Chief announced the following as said committee: Comrades E. F. M. Faehtz, of the Department of the Potomac; G. F. Potter, of the Department of New York; O. C. Bosbyshell, of the Department of Pennsylvania; James Shaw, Jr., of the Department of Rhode Island, and James W. Denny, of the Department of Massachusetts.

The investigation of the matter was thus placed in good and competent hands, and there is no doubt that any plan ultimately adopted will be one that will be safely guarded, economical in its operation, profitable as may be to the members, and the benefits of which will be mainly, if not exclusively, bestowed on the soldiers of the G. A. R., and their surviving widows.

MEMORIAL SERVICES,

DEPARTMENT OF MICHIGAN,

MAY, 1869.

————◆————

While the beautiful, touching and appropriate custom of adorning the graves of departed friends with wreaths and flowers has existed among men, time immemorial, the honor of establishing a DECORATION DAY, as an annual NATIONAL COMMEMORATION of the services, sacrifices, sufferings and death of the fallen soldiers of our country, belongs to the Grand Army of the Republic, and was instituted in compliance with the following GENERAL ORDER:

HEADQUARTERS GRAND ARMY OF THE REPUBLIC,
Adjutant General's Office, 446 Fourteenth Street,
WASHINGTON, D. C., May 5, 1868.

GENERAL ORDERS
No. 11.

I. The 30th day of May, 1868, is designated for the purpose of strewing with flowers or otherwise decorating the graves of Comrades who died in defense of their country during the late rebellion, and whose bodies now lie in almost every city, village, and hamlet church-yard in the land. In this observance no form of ceremony is prescribed, but Posts and Comrades will in their own way arrange such fitting services and testimonials of respect as circumstances may permit.

We are organized, Comrades, as our Regulations tell us, for the purpose, among other things, "of preserving and strengthening those kind and fraternal feelings which have bound together the soldiers, sailors, and marines who united to suppress the late rebellion." What can aid more to assure this result than by cherishing tenderly the memory of our heroic dead, who made their breasts a barricade between our country and its foes? Their soldier lives were the reveille of freedom to a race in chains and their deaths the tattoo of rebellious tyranny in arms. We should guard their graves with sacred vigilance. All that the consecrated wealth and taste of the nation can add to their adornment and security, is but a fitting tribute to the memory of her slain defenders. Let no wanton foot tread rudely on such hallowed grounds. Let pleasant paths invite the coming and going of reverent visitors and fond mourners. Let no vandalism of avarice or neglect; no ravages of time testify to the present or to the coming generations, that we have forgotten as a people the cost of a free and undivided Republic.

If other eyes grow dull, and other hands slack, and other hearts cold in the solemn trust, ours shall keep it well as long as the light and warmth of life remain to us.

Let us, then, at the time appointed gather around their sacred remains and garland the passionless mounds above them, with the choicest flowers of spring-time; let us raise above them the dear old flag they saved from dishonor; let us in this solemn presence renew our pledges to aid and assist those whom they have left among us a sacred charge upon a nation's gratitude,—the soldier's and sailor's widow and orphan.

II. It is the purpose of the Commander-in-Chief to inaugurate this observance with the hope that it will be kept up from year to year, while a survivor of the war remains to honor the memory of his departed Comrades. He earnestly desires the public press to call attention to this Order, and lend its friendly aid in bringing it to the notice of Comrades in all parts of the country, in time for simultaneous compliance therewith.

III. Department Commanders will use every effort to make this Order effective.

By order of—

JOHN A. LOGAN,
Commander-in-Chief.
N. P. CHIPMAN,
Adjutant General.

OFFICIAL:
WM. S. COLLINS, *A. A. G.*

The success which attended its observance in 1868, the beauty and effectiveness of the ceremony, and the high esteem and tender regard which already attaches to the THIRTIETH DAY OF MAY, as a day of remembrance of the nation's dead, has fixed it forever in the hearts of the American people as a National Anniversary, taking rank with the anniversary of our country's independence.

The memorial services which occurred this year throughout the United States, were held in obedience to the following GENERAL ORDER:

HEADQUARTERS GRAND ARMY OF THE REPUBLIC,
Adjutant General's Office, 411 F Street,
WASHINGTON, D. C., April 12, 1869.

GENERAL ORDERS }
No. 21. }

I. The 30th day of May proximo—a day set apart by the Grand Army of the Republic to commemorate the glorious deeds of our departed comrades—will be observed throughout the United States in such manner as befits the solemnities of the occasion, and as will testify the undying love of a grateful people for the memory of those who died that the nation might live.

This is the second public observance of the occasion, which is trusted will recur yearly while there remains a heart loyal to the cause in which our comrades fell, and while the moving principle of that struggle is worth preserving. If our organization had no other object, that alone of keeping green the resting-places of our nation's defenders, by this annual commemoration, would be motive enough to hold us together in a fraternal band.

The Commander-in-Chief desires to thank those patriotic men and women who gave their aid and sympathy on a former occasion to make successful this National Memorial day, and they are cordially invited to unite with the comrades of the Grand Army in the approaching ceremonies; and he thanks the loyal Press everywhere, through whose generous aid a lasting record has been made of the observances one year ago. To the Congress of the United States, the comrades are specially indebted for authorizing the publication, in book form, of the proceedings of last May, and for the promise held out that each year a compilation will be made and published, as a national recognition of sympathy with these memorial observances.

II. It has been determined not to prescribe any form of ceremony for universal observance, but each Post, or any number of Posts, may arrange together such fitting services as circumstances will permit. Department Commanders will use every effort to perfect arrangements for the occasion. The newspaper Press are requested to give publication to this order.

III. Department and Post Commanders are specially enjoined to preserve and forward to these Headquarters a copy of the proceedings (in printed form so far as possible) which take place in carrying out this order.

IV. As the 30th day of May occurs on Sabbath, Posts are at liberty to observe either that day, or Saturday, the 29th.

By order of—

JOHN A. LOGAN,
Commander-in-Chief.

N. P. CHIPMAN,
Adjutant General.

OFFICIAL:
WM. T. COLLINS, *A. A. G.*

———

In accordance with the above, the following General Order was issued by the Department of Michigan:

HEADQUARTERS DEPARTMENT OF MICHIGAN,)
Grand Army of the Republic,
LANSING, Mich., April 29, 1869.)

GENERAL ORDERS)
No. 3.)

I. The attention of Commanders of Posts of the Grand Army of the Republic, within the Department of Michigan, is called to General Orders No. 11 and 21—current series,—from General Headquarters.

II. Though the day designated on which to commemorate the deeds and revive the memories of our fallen comrades, occurs on Sabbath, thus leaving it optional with the Posts to observe that or some other day, yet it is recommended by the Grand Commander of this Department, that the 30th day of May—the day set apart by the Grand Army of the Republic for that purpose—be observed by the Posts within the Department, in such manner as to each shall seem befitting the day consecrated to the memory of comrades who gave their lives that the nation might live, the Union be preserved, our free institutions transmitted unimpaired, and liberty secured to the citizens of our loved Republic.

III. No form of ceremony for the day is prescribed. It is, however, recommended to the Posts within this Department—

1. That they request the clergymen within their respective limits to deliver a discourse during the day, (morning or evening,) adapted to the occasion ;

2. That the ceremonies and services at the cemeteries be of a character unexceptional to the Sabbath ;

3. That at the cemeteries ceremonies take place throughout the State, at 3 o'clock P. M. of the day designated.

IV. Grateful for the aid extended, and the sympathy manifested by the patriotic people of the State on the first observance of its MEMORIAL DAY, the Commander of the Department cordially invites all such to again join with the Grand Army of the Republic, in its annual visit to and decoration of the resting places of its departed comrades, and to participate in the ceremonies commemorating their glorious deeds.

V. Clergymen, in communities where a Post of the Grand Army of the Republic has not yet been organized, are requested to deliver a discourse during the MEMORIAL DAY adapted to the occasion, and the citizens of such localities are cordially invited, and respectfully urged to arrange together for such services and ceremonies on that day as to them shall seem a fitting expression of their sympathy with these observances and of their appreciation of the patriotic services of those whose deeds we commemorate.

VI. It is trusted that Post Commanders will give early attention to perfecting arrangements for the occasion, and that they will, as soon as such arrangements are perfected, forward to these Headquarters, a copy thereof, and also, at as early a day as practicable, a copy of all the proceedings connected with the execution of this order.

VII. The papers of the State will confer a favor by publishing this order.

By order of—

WM. HUMPHREY,

Grand Commander, Department of Michigan.

H. H. DANIELS, *Ass't Adj't Gen'l.*

4

The following is a summary of the Memorial Services held in the Department of Michigan, so far as information concerning them could be obtained by the compiler of this work:

ADRIAN.

The day appointed by Post Woodbury, for the observance of the Memorial Services, was Sunday, May 30th, but owing to the inclemency of the weather, they were postponed till Monday, May 31st.

The "Assembly" was sounded at 3½ P. M., in front of the Post Headquarters, and simultaneously with its sounding, the places of business were generally closed, as if by common consent. The streets began to fill with people, and as if to encourage a general turn-out, the sun shone out with more clearness than it had vouchsafed for some days. Shortly after 4 P. M., the procession was formed under the direction of Capt. Rogers, Commandant of Post Woodbury, G. A. R., assisted by his Adjutant, Major Simpson, and Messrs. Baker, Bowen and Westerman, as aids. The following was the order of procession:

BAND,
Mayor and Common Council of the City,
Clergy of the City,
Orator, Chaplain, and Department Commander,
CHOIR,
Girls, Dressed in White, in Carriages,
Wagon, loaded with Flowers,
Knights Templars,
Post Woodbury, G. A. R.,
German Workingmen's Benevolent Association,
Masonic Fraternity,
Odd Fellows,
Citizens.

The procession moved to the excellent music of the band up Broad street to Butler, east along Butler to Clinton, up Clinton to Hunt, along Hunt to Locust, and up Locust to the Cemetery. Arrived at the Cemetery, the procession moved through to the square, where the exercises opened by singing a hymn by the choir, consisting of Messrs. Bliss and Rice, Miss Mattie Graves and Mrs. J. H. Cole.

Prayer by Post Chaplain Hadley followed, which was succeeded by singing by the choir.

EXTRACTS FROM THE ORATION, BY CAPT. J. H. FEE.

Comrades of the Grand Army of the Republic, and friends:— Again we have assembled in these grounds, consecrated to the dead, to pay tribute to the memory of those who laid down their lives during the peril of the Nation, and of those who, after coming back to home and loved ones, have passed from our midst. We have not come here through mere curiosity to see what may be done, but each one, I trust, actuated by a deep, grateful love for the memory of, not only the dead heroes whose remains have been gathered in these beautiful grounds, but of the thousands of others who fell in the conflict, and a desire to give some tangible evidence of that love and gratitude.

These ceremonies which we have met to observe, in themselves beautiful and touchingly impressive, are most to be prized for the influence they exert upon the hearts and purposes of those who may take part in them. By our presence here we say that the cause in which these dead heroes died is one dear to us, and that while we thus strew the early flowers of spring-time over their resting places, we will keep green in our memories the noble work they did, and consecrate ourselves anew to the maintenance of the principles for the perpetuity of which they gave their lives. If there were no higher motive to influence us, gratitude to those who fell while fighting to assure the supremacy of that flag so beloved by the friends of liberty the world over, ought to be strong enough to make us regard their resting places as sacred, to be religiously guarded against all desecration.

All that we can do, or say, cannot affect our dead comrades. Their lives have been glorified. History will embalm their

deeds, and the people of the future will point, with pride, to
what these heroes did, while the words of others will have
been forgotten as not worthy of record. But so long as the
people of the United States shall prize, as they should, the
value of the services of our patriot dead, certainly so long as
there shall be a member of the Grand Army left, thus long
will tribute be paid to the memory of those whose lives made
up the price paid for the salvation of all that is worth preserving in our form of Government.

*   *   ,   *   *   *   *   *   *   *

But it is not to the dead alone that we owe gratitude.

> " * * * To those who, crippled, pine,
> Let us give hope of happier days.
> Let homes for all those sad wrecks of war
> Through all the land with speed arise ;
> They cry from every gaping scar,
> " Let not one brother's tomb debar
> The wounded living from your eyes ! ' ' '

These "sad wrecks of war" meet us in every avenue of society. Empty sleeves, and crutches, are painfully common
sights. These cripples are left among us, as it were, to test
the sincerity of our patriotic professions. To pay homage to
the dead, requires little or no sacrifice; but to do justice to the
living, implies the liberal expenditure of the means that, in
Providence, have been placed at our disposal. Words are
well, so far as they go, but if they are not backed up by generous deeds they do but little credit to him who utters them.
It is fitting on this occasion, when we have come together to
express our feeling for the dead, that we should look into our
own lives and see whether we are doing what we ought to do
for the living. There is no class of men who better deserve
our regard and care than these cripples, who came out of the
flame of battle, maimed for life. They fought, not for themselves alone, but for you and for me, and because they thus
fought, you and I owe them a debt, not only of gratitude, but
of a more tangible form; a debt which, in its honest payment,
will give them food to eat, clothes to wear, and for those who
have not home and friends, a home to live in. Not all the

maimed need this care and provision for their wants, but there is many a poor, crippled soldier who has no friend to whom he can go, save the people whom he so fairly served; and if that people heeds not his appeals, he must be indeed forsaken. There are institutions now springing up whose sole purpose is to seek out and gather in these "battle wrecks." There are at least three such now in successful operation, and if they be not sufficient to meet the demands made upon them, I have faith to believe that yet more ample provision will be made.

There are yet two other classes to whom the loyal people of the Nation owe a duty. that they cannot, will not, be so ungrateful as to neglect. These are the widows and orphans of those who laid down their lives on the altar of their country. In many and many an instance, the families of dead soldiers were left in want. They could secure only the commonest necessities of life by the hardest toil and closest economy when all were in health; but when sickness came, God alone knows the silent and uncomplaining suffering from cold and hunger that has been endured by these bereaved ones. Because they made no sign of their distress, those outside have thoughtlessly paid no heed to them, or, if they were forced to see the misery, they had no mode of relief to suggest other than the "Poor House;" and because a soldier's widow has refused to allow her children to be gathered in with common paupers, she has been called proud. Well, she has cause to be proud; for as the widow of a brave man who fell fighting for liberty, she is better entitled to the praise and esteem of men worthy of freedom than the proudest queen.

It is a duty we owe to the dead to see that those who depended upon them receive all needful support, and when we stop short of this, we fail of discharging the most sacred obligations that can be put upon us. In many of the States provisions are being made for the education of the children of dead soldiers. In several, this movement has been so far prosecuted that the schools have been established and the children gathered together. To the Grand Army of the Republic belongs the credit of initiating this measure, but to the credit of the people be it said, that the work of these representatives of our Grand Armies has been warmly seconded by the Legislatures, in granting generous appropriations. The duty we owe to the children of our dead soldiers is imperative. These children are fast growing up, and what we do must be done quickly. In a few years they will be beyond our reach. The immediate question to be settled is, shall they grow up in ignorance, among the degrading influences that surround them in our streets, or shall they have, what they have a perfect right to demand, a good education? Michigan has done nothing in this direction yet, but the time is not far off when she will have the opportunity to place herself right in this matter. The comrades of these sleeping heroes have determined that justice shall be done these little ones. They will initiate the work, and the State will be appealed to for assistance, and I shall be much mistaken if the appropriation to carry out this worthy object be not one of the most popular that our representatives can vote.

*　　*　　*　　*　　*　　*　　*　　*　　*

Among an ancient people it was the custom immediately after a victorious battle to rear a trophy, which was but a heap made up by casting together the arms and spoils captured from the enemy. These trophies were regarded as sacred, and no one dared to tear them down; and when through time they decayed and crumbled, no one was permitted to rebuild them. Plutarch, in speaking of this, ascribes a praiseworthy motive to the people observing the custom, for, says he, " to reinstate, and set up again the monuments of ancient differences with enemies, which time has conveniently demolished, has something odious in it, and seems to argue a desire to perpetuate enmity." The trophies that we set up on our victorious battle fields are fast crumbling, but many good men are questioning whether we ought not to rebuild them. To rebuild is to perpetuate enmity, which, as Plutarch says, " has something odious in it." Rather let our trophies crumble down into forgetfulness if thus our people may be brought into unity and harmony. This implies no sacrifice of principle or worthy purpose, but simply the exercise of a broad charity which, while it carries buckler and shield for defense of the Nation, has a warm hand for those who yield willing obedience to the laws of the land.

When enmity shall have given way to friendship, when trust shall have taken the place of distrust, when we shall become indeed one people, then will our Nation make such advancement as the most sanguine has not dreamed of. When we shall enter upon the fruition of the work so nobly begun by the men for whom the spring has to-day given up its earliest buds and flowers, let us not forget that what we enjoy, are blessings won by them and passed into our keeping as a sacred legacy, which it is our duty to preserve and keep intact so long as we have the capacity to appreciate, or a memory to cherish their sacrifices.

During his address the speaker presented the subject of erecting a monument to the departed soldiers, stating that the national government had donated to the city a splendid shaft of white marble, for that purpose. A subscription was raised sufficient to build a pedestal, carve the names, and set up and complete the monument.

At the close of the oration a hymn was sung, and this was succeeded by the ceremony of decorating the graves. The following is a list of the soldiers whose graves were decorated, with their rank and command, so far as we could ascertain them:

Major Chas. Hoyt, 15th infantry.
James Stebbins, 17th infantry.
Ada Bradish, 2d infantry.
Daniel G. Washburn, Co. E, 1st Mo.
Robert Miller, 8th infantry.
Serg't Alfred M. Smith, 18th infantry.
Col. D. A. Woodbury, 4th infantry.

Capt. F. Ladd, 9th cavalry.
Col. L. L. Comstock, 17th infantry.
Col. W. Huntington Smith, 20th infantry.
Thos. Kline, 18th infantry, Co. C.
Capt. Alonzo M. Rogers, Co. A, 1st Ga. infantry U. S. A.
Serg't H. E. McLouth, Co. F, 4th Mich. cavalry.
Orrin B. McLouth, Co. F, 4th Mich. cavalry.
E. D. Thompson, Co. C, 18th infantry.
Orrin M. Smith.
R. J. Clegg, Co. G, 4th infantry.
Alexander Oughletree, Co. B, 18th infantry.
Jehiel Lossing.
Col. L. S. Elliott, 49th Ohio infantry.
Fred. Hall.
Lieut. W. L. Osborn, 9th cavalry.
J. E. Seamons, Co. F, 4th Mich cavalry.
D. G. E. Peck.
Edward Kingsley, 1st infantry.
Melan W. Coats, 12th infantry.
James W. Sherman, 26th infantry.
Julian Morey, 1st infantry.
Chas. Loomis.

Every thing connected with the ceremonies passed off in the most pleasant and satisfactory manner. The procession presented a fine appearance, fully the equal of any ever seen in the city, the streets along the line of march were lined with people, and an immense crowd, variously estimated at from three to five thousand, was collected inside the grounds of the cemetery. There were flowers in profusion, and the comrades of Post Woodbury can congratulate themselves that everything passed off so satisfactorily, and that the people at large paid so high a tribute of respect to the memory of their dead comrades.

33

ANN ARBOR.

Saturday, May 29th, 1869, was observed as a Memorial Day by the citizens of Ann Arbor, and the business houses were generally closed. It was a day befitting the occasion. It did not rain, but the face of the sun was hid from view by a vail of clouds, and the whole heavens seemed clad in garments of sympathetic sorrow.

The opening exercises were held in the court-house square, commencing at 9 o'clock A. M. First, Vocal Music—"My Country,"—which the audience joined in singing. Second, Prayer—by the Rev. Mr. Gillespie. This was an eloquent, appropriate, and patriotic invocation for our common country, and a devout expression of gratitude and thankfulness for the salvation of free institutions and a good government. Third, an

ADDRESS BY PRESIDENT E. O. HAVEN,

of Michigan University, who spoke, in substance, as follows:

We are assembled, not to re-open the wounds of our late contest, though I wonder not at the tears in many an eye started by the pathetic song just sung so eloquently, nor can we fail to feel that this is a solemn occasion. We are participating in what may claim to be almost a national celebration. From Maine to Oregon, from Michigan to Florida—yes, even in the South, flowers will be strewn over the graves of the heroes who gave up their lives for their country. In olden times this custom prevailed—it prevails still in Europe; but there were never so many people participating at once in this ceremony as to-day. We would not revive the agony of the past struggle, but we cannot, we will not forget the heroes that died for us.

There comes a time in the life of every person when the buoyancy of childhood is exchanged for the stability and earnestness of manhood. It may be some tremendous misfortune, the treachery of a friend, or the advent of some responsibility,

5

that revolutionizes and improves our life. So is it with nations. Every nation, to improve its metal, must be tried as by
fire. Now, America was a gay and thoughtless child a few
years ago, compared with her present sobriety and steady,
noble character.

The old Revolutionary war was fearful, but it had been almost forgotten. The war of 1812 was a mere fight at sea; the
Mexican affair was an adventure participated in by a few; but
our late struggle was an .awful contest for existence. There
were times when the best and strongest feared that death
would be the issue; but the Arbiter of Nations, the God of
battles, did not so decide. He has declared, America shall
live.

I shall not discuss the contest. I shall utter no words of
censure. It was first a war of ideas and words, and finally a
war of physical strength and military science. Now let us
have peace. Now, as God has decided that as this great world-
nation is one in geography and one in language, (though
speaking many,) it shall be one in government, and have one
flag, let us repel and discourage differences, and seek to be
truly one. Every part of the nation contributed to the result.
From our own city many enlisted, and many lost their lives in
the contest. Their names, though not yet chiseled in marble
or wrought in brass, shall never perish. They shall yet be inscribed on memorials as. imperishable as anything human.
They are written in the memories of grateful friends.

These flowers are beautiful. They are representatives of the
divine wisdom and love. They are created only to please.
They are perishable, but they perpetually return. So our
emotions are fleeting, but the fountain of emotion and thought
is imperishable. Let these flowers, then, be placed over the
mortal remains of our heroes. And while we pay to them our
highest tribute of respect and love, let us not forget the many
who sleep far away from us in unknown graves. Perhaps
some stranger hands to-day will ornament their graves. If

not, the angels know where they are. God has not forgotten them. We will not forget them.

Fallen heroes, are you with us to-day? Then all hail! Full well ye know your labors were not in vain, and you have your reward. Your country lives because you died for it, and you have earned immortal honor. Your memory is a benediction. Exult, then, in your immortality, while we in our earthly life take the best emblems of Heaven we have, the blossoms of God's beauty, and spread them over the spots where your bodies repose—faint emblems of our undying love. You have not died in vain. Your country is saved; other countries shall imitate it, and the world shall yet be a family of Republics!

At the close of the address there was singing by the quartette, and the benediction was pronounced by Rev. Mr. Gillespie.

After the exercises in the square, the procession was formed in the following order:

1st. Officers of the day.
2d. Mayor and Officers of the City Government.
3d. Band with Muffled Drums.
4th. National Colors Draped.
5th. Porter Zouaves with Arms Reversed.
6th. Soldiers with Bouquets.
7th. Masons and Odd Fellows.
8th. Fire Department Officers.
9th. Celtic Literary Society.
10th. Citizens on foot and in Carriages.

The Porter Zouaves made a fine appearance, under the command of Captain Porter. They have the air and bearing of men who have seen actual service, smelt gun-powder, and heard bullets whistle. The Band also in the morning gave some excellent music.

In the above order the procession moved to Forest Hill Cemetery, where, upon its arrival, the ceremony of strewing the graves with flowers was commenced. The following is the list of deceased soldiers, whose graves were decorated:

36

FOREST HILL CEMETERY.

Capt. Edward H. Gilbert,
Lieut. Amos M. Ladd,
Lieut. Nelson Imus,
John S. Farnell,
Henry C. Ide,
Capt. L. E. Holden,
Harry G. Weed,
Edward L. Grover,
Francis M. Clark,
Clarkson Pack,
—— Reed,
William C. Loomis,
George D. H. Cowles,
Wilbur F. Bartlit,

Lieut. William A. Brown,
Jesse Hyde,
Jonas D. Richardson,
Col. Norval E. Welch,
Capt. Horace V. Knight,
Lieut. Aaron C. Jewett,
Charles L. Mills,
Capt. Wendell D. Wiltsie,
Henry Mowerson,
Augustus Helber,
Chaplain J. Blanchard,
John R. Wilcoxson,
Charles Gartner.

OLD CEMETERY.

James Felch,

Henry Bierman.

LOWER TOWN CEMETERY.

Lieut. George Williams,
John Smith,

Maj. John M. Randolph.

ST. THOMAS' CEMETERY.

William Champion,
William H. Stephens,
Cornelius Sheehan,

John Hogan,
Duffee Duquette.

The following are names of those whose bodies lie on battle fields, in unknown graves, or are buried in Southern cemeteries. The list is incomplete, but is made as full as possible:

Capt. R. G. Depue,
Maj. Henry S. Burnett,
Sergt. Maj. F. Kingsley,
George W. Huson,
Sergt. Jared Pond,
Sergt. Geo. B. Felch,
Capt. R. P. Carpenter,
. Geo. Traker,
Sergt. D. E. Ainsworth,
Capt. Walter McCollum.

Frederick Corselius,
Corp. Abram Romig,
Jacob Neithamer,
Clark C. Briggs,
Myron J. Gillespie,
John Garrison,
William P. Lovejoy,
John Weekly,
Capt. Oliver Blood, Jr.,
Frank Fisher,

Geo. Vanderwarker,
Capt. Henry C. Arnold,
William Nichols,
Geo. Gaunt,
Sergt. David C. Holmes,
Lieut. W. W. Burch,
Andrew Britton,
Orson L. Giles,
Geo. W. Barber,
Michael Kean,

Byron Cook,
Sergt. Edward P. Clark,
Fred. Wildt,
John McCarty,
Geo. C. Mead,
Lawrence Norton,
Patrick McCourt,
John Shannon,
Henry Spoor.

An eye-witness furnishes the following touching *incidents* of the scene:

It was a beautiful sight to see the old comrades who had stood with them shoulder to shoulder in the storm of leaden and iron hail, amid the shouts of victory, and the groans of the wounded and dying, strewing the graves of these Dead Heroes with beautiful flowers—the tokens of God's love, and the evidences of His wisdom—in memory of their worth and the service they rendered their country.

We noticed that the relations and perhaps more immediate friends lingered around these graves after the procession had moved on; and we lingered too. By these mourners we saw the most touching tributes offered over the graves of our fallen dead—the lamented, the loved, and the lost! These lingering mourners strewed over the graves of their loved ones, rose-buds, evergreens, myrtle, and all the bright and beautiful gems of Flora's magnificent bower, bright, fresh, beautiful, fragrant, and unfading—the flowers of *memory*, all bedewed with the tears of affection. Shall I say it? Most of these mourners were women. God bless them. They are, after all, "the cream, the sparkle, the elixir," of this life. We saw a little group gathered, as we supposed, over the mortal remains of some noble soul, but as we drew near, we found that it was a spot sacred to the memory of " Frank Kingsley, 1st Sergeant, Company H, 20th Michigan Infantry, and acting Sergeant Major, killed in the battle of Spotsylvania Court House, May 12, 1864," whose body was never found. But the hands of affection—whether those of father, brother, sister, or lover, or all combined, we know not—had anticipated the procession in decorating this spot. In a neat little case with a glass front, we saw the following beautiful little tribute to his memory, entwined, as was fitting, with a beautiful wreath of flowers and evergreens:

" Since treason sought our country's heart,
   Ah! Fairer body never yet
From noble soul was torn apart,
   No braver blood has wet
           Her Coronet.

No spirit more intense and fierce,
   Strove where her starry banner waves,
No gentler face beloved, than thine,
   Sleeps in a Soldier's grave;
           No heart more brave.

And though his mound I may not trace,
   Or weep above his buried head,
The grateful Spring shall find the place,
   And with her blossoms spread
           His quiet bed."

BATTLE CREEK.

Decoration Services were observed at Battle Creek, on Sunday, May 30, 1869.

In the forenoon, the Rev. Mr. Wishard, at the Congregational and Presbyterian church, preached an able sermon suitable to the day, from the text, Acts xxii, 28: "With a great sum obtained I this freedom." The discourse set forth the cost of our national liberties, with some very practical hints in regard to the best method of preserving them.

Notwithstanding the storm which prevailed on that day, quite a large number of citizens assembled at the Methodist Episcopal Church, at 2 o'clock P. M., and proceeded thence to the Cemetery for the purpose of decorating with flowers, the graves of our deceased soldiers, and witnessing the exercises which were to be observed in commemoration of the brave men buried there, who had given their lives in the service of their country.

Upon arriving at the stand, Dr. S. S. French, Surgeon of the 20th Mich. Infantry, who presided, and read the names of those whose remains had been deposited in the Cemetery, called the assembly to order. An appropriate prayer was offered by Chaplain L. W. Earl. We give a few

EXTRACTS FROM THE ORATION OF HON. CHAS. S. MAY.

On this last Christian Sabbath of the Spring, the nation, by the hands of their comrades in life, lays its floral offering on the graves of its dead. No day is too sacred for such a beautiful and impressive service—a service most fit and appropriate also, for these flowers are emblems of resurrection and immortality.

It is a service which answers to a universal sentiment felt in all lands and times. National gratitude for national and patriotic labors and sacrifices, has found expression in the highest forms of human speech and the noblest creations of human art. Poetry and eloquence have combined to do honor to those who died for liberty and country. When the Athenians would honor the dead who fell in disastrous battle for the Republic, at Cheronea, they chose Demosthenes, the Prince of orators, to pronounce the oration over their sacred ashes, and that majestic eulogy still kindles the emulation of orators and fires the heart of patriotism.

A poet of our mother land (Collins), at a comparatively recent day, has embalmed this sentiment in immortal verse:

" How sleep the brave who sink to rest
By all their country's wishes blest ?
When Spring, with dewy fingers cold,
Returns to deck their hallowed mold,
She there shall dress a sweeter sod
Than Fancy's feet have ever trod :

" There Freedom comes, a pilgrim gray,
To bless the turf that wraps the clay ;
And honor shall awhile repair,
To dwell, a weeping hermit, there."

We owe this tribute to the dead. We cannot forget their great service to us and the nation. That service was undertaken in full view of all its perils and dangers, but these young men did not stop to count the cost. Fired by an ardent and noble patriotism, they went forth to battle and to death, and have won the crown of martyrdom.

While sharing the common sentiment, and paying the common honor to the great host who fell, our immediate tribute to-day is to the dead of this city and its vicinity. Their names, and their honorable titles won in the war have just been read in your hearing. Many of these men I knew; some were among my most valued personal friends. I would not be invidious in such a presence, but I recall among these latter, the names of Rhines, of Byington, of Mason, of Barnes and Knight, and Galpin—many others equally worthy, you knew and honored.

How shall I speak of the great and memorable results and fruits of the sacrifice which these men made for their country? A Union restored, a land redeemed and regenerated, liberty perpetuated—these are some of them. And not among the least of the results of the war is that great and immortal example of patriotism which is left for the glory of our country and the emulation of all our posterity. I sometimes think that this is the richest fruit of the struggle, and that it outweighs in solid value the more material results which we seem first to appreciate. For is it not such riches that give to nations their highest glory and strength?

Greater, and more to be valued, is this splendid example of patriotism than even our re-cemented bands of Union, than the strength of our army on the land, and our navy on the sea, than all our commerce, or all our vast material resources and wealth. It was PATRIOTISM that nerved the arms of these our heroes; LOVE OF COUNTRY,—that same lofty sentiment that inspired Leonidas and the three hundred, when they made that immortal sacrifice in the pass of Thermopylæ—that lent wings of fire to the eloquence of Demosthenes, matchless and unrivaled still in all the ages, that, centuries later, gave courage to the Swiss patriot Winkelreid, when he cried, "Make way for Liberty!" and gathered the Austrian spears in his bosom;—that has inspired and cheered a noble army of heroes and martyrs who, in many lands and in all ages, on field and scaffold, have laid down their lives that their country might live!

We owe this service to ourselves. We should be unworthy of the political liberty purchased by these sacrifices, and the glorious land enriched by such blood, if we did not cherish in our heart of hearts the memory of these brave men. We are exalted when we exalt and honor public virtue and devotion like this. Nations are lifted up by services and sentiments of gratitude and honor for their benefactors.

In these dead are planted the noble germs of future patriots and martyrs who will defend this country as they so signally and successfully defended it, if ever occasion should come again.

I cannot put in the poor forms of speech the feelings of these fathers who stand to-day with us over the graves of their sons. But this I can say to them: Fathers, you should be proud and thankful that God gave you such sons. Death will soon come to us all. A few more years of toil and care and vicissitude, and all this throng of the living standing here above these graves of the dead, shall mingle their dust with those who have gone before. And is it not a consolation to these friends; is it not a real felicity to the departed, that for a few years of common life these heroic young men were able to write their

6

names on the immortal roll, and share the enduring fame of the defenders of country, and the martyrs of liberty?

In the midst of peace and prosperity; at the opening dawn of a new career for our country, we strew these flowers upon the graves of our heroes. Let it be a service that shall never be forgotten, as the unfolding years of the new·time roll on; let it hereafter be one of the sacred days of the Republic. This is now a land of liberty and law. Following swiftly after our victories in war, which restored the Union and consolidated our nationality, are our recent great victories of peace. The Atlantic and the Pacific are now joined together, and the great oceans themselves are no longer barriers to our progress. And above these great material triumphs the Genius of our new civilization points with majestic wand to the still more glorious prospects and achievements of the future, when on this noble continent—the most splendid theatre of action God ever gave to nation or people—a hundred millions of free and enlightened Americans shall work out the dream of the fathers of the Republic, and illustrate the noblest conception of national power and civilization.

Sleep on, noble dead; the nation shall not forget you. It is your sacrifices and blood that make possible the realization of hopes so magnificent.

" In the still camps of death
The comrades of your toils and tramps lie,
And marble sentries guard, with noiseless breath,
Their green encampments of eternity."

The following is a list of comrades buried in the Cemetery of Batte Creek:

Gen. W. H. Revere entered the service in April, 1861, as a Lieutenant in the New York Fire Zouaves; served during the rebellion and died in command of the post at Morehead City, North Carolina, September 20th, 1865.

Maj. C. Byington entered the service in April, 1861, as Captain of Company C, 2d Michigan Infantry, and died in December, 1863, in consequence of wounds received at the siege of Knoxville, Tennessee.

Col. Geo. C. Barnes, entered the service in August, 1862, as Captain of

Company C, 20th Michigan Infantry, and was killed in front of Petersburgh, Va., June 18th, 1864.

Captain George C. Knights entered the service in August, 1862, as Lieutenant in the 1st Michigan Sharpshooters, was killed in front of Petersburg, June 17th, 1864.

Lieut. Charles Brown entered the service in August, 1862, as Lieutenant of Company C, 20th Mich. Infantry, and died of disease contracted in the field early in 1863.

Lieut. Timothy Fish entered the service in April, 1861, as a Corporal in Company C, 2d Michigan Infantry; served four years, and died of wounds received at Petersburg, April 2d, 1865.

Lieut. Albert Barney entered the service in August, 1862, as a Private in Company C, 20th Michigan Infantry, and died from wounds received at or near Coal Harbor, Va., June 1st, 1864.

Lieut. Geo. B. Hicks entered the service in August, 1862, as a Sergeant of Company C, 20th Michigan Infantry, and was killed in front of Petersburg, June 18th, 1864.

Miles R. Sherman entered the service in August, 1861, as a Private in Company H, Merrill's Horse, and died from wounds received in battle near Memphis, Missouri, July 18th, 1862.

Ebenezer Jones entered the service as a Private in Company I, Merrill's Horse, in August, 1861, and was killed in battle near Memphis, Missouri, July 18th, 1862.

James M. Shaver, record not known to the committee.

Franklin Davis entered the service early in the rebellion, and died from disease contracted in the service. The particulars of his record are not known to the committee.

John McCamly entered the service as a private in Company H, Merrill's Horse, and died of disease contracted in the line of his duty, at Nashville, Tenn., in 1865.

Peter Stevens, a Private in the 54th Massachusetts regiment. Mortally wounded at the assault on Fort Wagner.

Thomas Fuller entered the service in February, 1865, and died near Harper's Ferry, in May, 1865.

Palmer Pugsley entered the service in April, 1861, as a Private in Company C, 2d Michigan Infantry, and died in Virginia early in 1862.

Edwin and Edward Dumphrey, twin brothers, one killed in battle and the other died from wounds received in battle. The particulars of their enlistment and subsequent record not known to the committee.

Foster D. Miller entered the service in March, 1865, and died of disease contracted in the line of duty, near Lexington, Missouri, June 6th, 1865.

James A. Barnum, entered the service in August, 1862, as a Private in

Company C, 20th Michigan Infantry, and died in hospital, of disease contracted in the line of duty, at Cincinnati, Ohio, June, 1863.

Four buried on Soldiers' Lot. Names and record unknown to the committee.

The following are among those who went from this place, and to-day fill unknown graves on the field where they fell :

Col. James B. Mason, entered the service in 1861, and fell in battle near Salt Springs, Va., October, 1864.

Maj. John Piper, entered the service in 1861, and fell at Spottsylvania, Va., May 12th, 1864.

Col. L. C. Rhines, fell in front of Petersburg, June 17th, 1864. Finally buried at Jackson, Michigan.

Lieut. F. Davis, killed at Marion, Virginia.

Lieut. Charles Galpin, entered the service in 1861, fell at the siege oï Knoxville, November, 1863.

BERRIEN SPRINGS.

EXTRACTS FROM THE ADDRESS OF CAPT. H. A. FORD.

Friends of the Soldier-dead:

It is a beautiful custom of the Irish people, in their native isle, to turn from the ways of business or of pleasure, and join for a time, however brief, the passing funeral procession. Whether he whom the mourning follow be friend or stranger, rich or poor, high or lowly born, it matters not; the tribute of respect is thought due and is paid to the sacred ashes of the dead. With something of this spirit do we gather here to-day. We have left the wonted duties and blessed repose of these hallowed hours. We have moved again to the slow, sad music of the funeral march. We have come to populate with tearful life this habitation of the lifeless, the home appointed for all living; to crown with wreaths, and chaplets, and garlands, these tombs by the hillside, where sweetly rest the feet that will tread no more the flowery meads of earth; to speak the words of praise above lips that are silent and ears that are dulled forever to the sounds of time.

We do honor this day to no common dust. In the throng of sleepers here are some whose memory we shall not willingly let die. They are the warrior-dead. They are the martyrs of a noble cause; the offerings of a nation's love and devotion to a grand principle; the dear sacrifices laid upon the altar of Liberty and country,—the slain of the great rebellion. Here, in the ranks of death, has been mustered your quota of the watchful guards of the rights of man and the unity of the nation, who died at their posts, with their armor on. In this tranquil solitude, after their toils, their vigils, their dangers, and their conflicts, they restfully slumber. "Till the heavens be no more, they shall not awake, nor be raised out of their sleep."

*　　*　　*　　*　　*　　*　　*　　*

Now and here, as perhaps never before, we may realize the truth of the classic line—made more classic for us by Warren than by Horace,—

"Sweet and fitting it is for one's country to die."

Our eyes range over a tract thickly underlaid with the remains of mortality. Death is the common lot. None escape. "It is appointed unto men once to die." But indeed—

"By few is Glory's wreath attained;
Though death or soon or late awaiteth all;
To *fight* in Freedom's cause is something gained,
And nothing lost—to FALL."

In the life of these, our heroes gone, there was especial merit; in their death, especial grandeur; in their memory there is claim for especial honor. Eight years ago this day they were with you and of you—strong, stalwart, full of ruddy life, already enjoying or standing upon the threshold of vigorous, hopeful, useful, manhood. To them, as to you, life was sweet, and home was dear. Just as pleasant to them were the sights and sounds and vocations of peace. These smiling fields, that fair and rich plateau, these circling woods, yon picturesque river vale, these billowy hills,—all spread away as beautiful to them as to us to-day. Just as blue were the heavens that bent above them; just as soft the late spring-days. But the call of country came, and they heard. The tools of husbandry and trade were dropped. The dearest ties of earth were sundered. Their most precious interests, in part, were sacrificed. Taking their lives in their hands, they went forth to do battle for God, for man, for fatherland. They went in a spirit not unlike that which animated the chivalrous Lasalle and his brave companions, the missionaries of Jesus, as they sailed with their strange company up yonder stream two hundred years ago, to advance the banner of civilization and plant the standard of the cross in these trackless wilds. With a valor and devotion to the safety of the State like that of Curtius in the old Roman story, they threw themselves, full-armed, into the chasm that threatened to engulf the Republic. They went to engage in no gigantic riot, no monstrous prize-fight, no strife of factions, no civil war in the old sense of "two opposing forces in the State contending in an irregular and violent way for the mastery, neither seeking to destroy the nation, but each, on the contrary, protesting their superior devotion to the preservation of the national life;" but they went to quell a rebellion against the principle of free government, to engage in a struggle for the nation's life, to put down a long-dominant oligarchy that was anti-national to the core. They went to suffer and to die that the nation might live. "Greater love hath no man than this, that he lay down his life for his friend."

Need I further follow the story of these unreturning brave? Alas! it is but too fresh in your memory. Their toils, their privations, their sufferings, their death—are not these written as with a pen of iron upon your very heart of hearts forever? Let this record suffice—they did their duty, and here, "after life's fitful fever, they sleep well."

A contest arduous and fierce as that through which they passed was likely to cost us the bravest and best. Never more true was the thought of Sophocles,

" War takes the noblest ever."

He who kept his feet most faithfully on the dragging march;

who performed most punctually his details, however laborious, in the camp and field; who most freely exposed himself on picket and in the severer lines of duty, was most open to the encroachments of disease, and most liable to fall an early victim to his fidelity. He who was prominent "on the perilous edge of battle, where it raged," was the readiest mark for the rifle's deadly aim. He who was boldest in the dangerous but important duty of the scout, the spy, the forager, was the likeliest to be made a captive, and to be ruthlessly shot down, or borne away to the scaffold, or, little better, to those awful prison-pens from which so few returned. Truly you may reckon the slumbering warriors here as of your bravest and your best, and worthiest of your honor. There were among you better men, perchance, in their daily lives. I know not how that may be. This I feel, that their faithful service and noble death have atoned for many an error, if such they made. Their self-sacrificing patriotism, like charity, has mantled a multitude of sins —at least in our memories, if not in the view of the Eternal Judge. "Death," says Bacon, "openeth the good fame, and extinguisheth envy." We shall recall, if we may not fully adopt, the generous sentiment of the old historian: "It is a debt of justice to pay superior honors to men who have devoted their lives in fighting for their country, though inferior to others in every virtue but that of valor; for, by their bravery, they obliterated the evil of their former lives, and the blessings which they conferred on the State were greater than the injuries which they had inflicted on private individuals."

"The whole earth," said Pericles, over the dead of the first Peloponnesian war, referring, doubtless, to the universality of their fame, "The whole earth is the sepulchre of illustrious men." To which another has added: "All time is the millennium of their glory." From the dawn of history, the homage of gratitude and admiration has been paid to the noble dead who have laid down their lives, that their fellow-men might be the safer and the happier. Wherever the better feelings of our nature have had sway, there high honors have been paid to the

warrior-dead. The monument of Absalom still stands in the
valley of the Kedron; the green mound of Patroclus yet adorns
the margin of the Trojan plain; the tomb of Themistocles has
looked out for two thousand years upon the placid waters of
the Grecian seas; the traveler may now see the long barrow
which a saved and grateful people erected over the fallen heroes at Marathon; while, in later ages, statues and tombs,
monuments, mausoleums, and memorial temples have been
made to dot the civilized world in memory of the patriot-slain.

*   *   *   *   *   *   *   *

Comrades of the Grand Army :—It has been our fortune to live
and bear part in the second of the heroic periods of American
history. For us, too, have been hunger and privation, heart-
sickness and home-sickness; the weary march, the camp and
bivouac, the front of battle, the headlong charge, the desperate
defense, the prison and the hospital—the "austere glory of
suffering" as did they who fought in the first war for the independence of the republic. As we stand in this peaceful spot,
on this holy day, in the garb of the citizen, we recall the Sab-
baths of toil and blood. We are again in the dust of the
marching columns, in the rifle-pits, the trenches, on the skir-
mish line, at the cannon's mouth, on the terrible raid. We
behold again the fated land as the garden of Eden before us,
and behind a desolate wilderness. We hear once more the
shriek of deadly missiles, the groan of the dying, the gay voices
of the camp, the thrilling notes that sound reveille or tattoo,
the advance or charge. We see the brilliant lines of the
parade or drill, and the ranks that form in battle's magnifi-
cently-stern array. We feel again the flush of the bivouac-fire
upon our cheeks, and see its light reflected from the manly
faces that surround it. We know, as others cannot, for what,
and how, these our fallen brothers suffered, fought, and fell.
The teachings of their lives are fully ours. By the beating
and the burning of our hearts, we feel their spirits with us to-
day. Above their sacred dust let us breathe an oath like that

of Demosthenes: "By those who met the peril at Marathon!—by those who formed the battle-line at Platæa!—by those who conquered in the sea-fight at Salamis!—by the men of Artemisium!—by the others, so many and so brave, who now rest in our public sepulchres!" or, better, an oath like Lincoln's, "registered in heaven," that so far as in us lies, the integrity of the Union and the rights of man SHALL FOREVER BE MAINTAINED. When the call of country comes again, we shall be ready. If the clouds that begin to lower above our land and the perfidious isle beyond the sea, should break in storm upon our heads, they shall find us at our posts of duty. With our comrades celebrating like obsequies yesterday, this day, and to-morrow, across the continent, we shall take care that the Republic receives no detriment. "Blessed be the Lord our strength, which teacheth our hands to war and our fingers to fight!"

Heaven grant, though, that war may not come again to this fair land. Earth has no loathlier sight than a battle-field. "Next to defeat," said Wellington, "the saddest thing is a victory." But let us take the truth to heart anew, my comrades, that while man lives and the earth endures, the heroic age of moral conflict is never past. Upon us still press the foes of man, of country, and of God. To us are yet committed great trusts, high duties, motive for noble deeds. Be vigilant, be brave, be true!

> "On! let all the soul within you
> For the truth's sake go abroad;
> Strike! let every nerve and sinew
> Tell for ages—tell for God!"

List of soldiers buried at Berrien Springs:

Wm. Dennison, Private Co. C, 25th Michigan Infantry.
—— Fancher.
Martin Gubby, Private 6th Michigan Artillery.
—— Horner.
Joel Kerr, Corporal Co. H, 26th Michigan Infantry.
H. J. Mastin.

J. B. Odell, Private Co. I, 12th Michigan Infantry.
Thomas Streets, "   "   "   "
John Tenant, Capt. Co. K,   "   "
Seri Trimm, Private Co. C, 25th   "   "
Joseph Vetter, Private Co. K, 12th " "
Miles Woods,   "   Co. H, 9th "   "

BUCHANAN.

The decoration of the soldiers' graves in Oak Ridge Cemetery, and the "Old Village Burying Ground," of Buchanan, took place on Sunday, May 30th, 1869. The ceremonies were solemn and imposing; the only unpleasant feature of the occasion being the stormy condition of the weather. However, the soldier boys, being used to all kinds of weather, heeded not the pelting rain, and sallied forth from their armory at two o'clock P. M., in uniform, accompanied by the B. C. Band, and proceeded to the Oak Grove Cemetery. From this time on to the close, the ceremonies were of the most impressive and solemn nature. The music by the band, (a mournful dirge), seemed to prepare all for the work before them, and, as it were, solemnized every heart, as they proceeded on their noble errand of true soldierly patriotism. The scene, upon arriving at the grave-yard, was one, also, that need long remain in the memories of those present, at least, those interested.

Upon arriving at the cemetery, a hollow square was formed by the soldiers, and the services opened with prayer by Eld. J. R. Berry, and reading of the Scriptures by the Chaplain of the Post. Post Commander B. E. Binns addressed the comrades in a brief and appropriate manner.

Officers and Soldiers of the Grand Army of the Republic:

In memory of the dead, and in behalf of friends, and in the name of our once blood-stained, and distorted, but now, happy and peaceful country, I greet you at the graves of your fallen comrades.

Your mission to this place, at this hour, is one of deep significance. The past, the present, and the future history of our country, all combine to add interest to the occasion, and it is in every way characteristic of a humane and Christian people.

In demonstration of respect for the dead, the American people are preëminent. Confessedly, there is no nation of the earth that pay more attention to, or hold in greater regard their dead, than the American people. Great care is taken in the selection and location of our cemeteries, and every effort made to make them places of beauty and attraction. Costly tombstones and marble monuments mark the resting places of the dead; and in many instances, memoirs, obituaries, and sometimes whole volumes are written concerning the life and death of the departed. This is well—it is right—it is but characteristic of our social, intellectual, and religious culture.

Your visit to-day to the graves of fallen soldiers of the Grand Army of the Republic, is one peculiar to itself—it has no parallel in history. Memory, faithful to her trust, re-produces the terrible and unnatural war through which we have passed. A thousand thoughts press themselves upon us, and come welling up for utterance. As we stand here to-day, we think of the long family quarrel, and bitter strife of words, that preceded the firing of the first shot upon that almost defenseless fort, the echo of which summoned a million of men to arms, and sent State dashing on State in fierce collision, drenched the land in fraternal blood, and unsettled the civilized world. The flag of our country was insulted—fire flashed in every eye, and blood flowed quick in every vein. This was followed by the shrill notes of the bugle-call, to arms! mingled with groans, and heart-throbs, and farewells at home; hunger, cold, and long, weary marches over unbeaten roads, through poison swamps, and all the hardships and dangers incident to army life, that make up the peculiar, unwritten history of the war, that must forever remain unwritten. The cause, as well as the effect of this great national drama, is, to my mind, most beautifully described in a poem written by George Lansing Taylor, and I cannot forbear quoting a stanza or two:

> "Crash, fell the thunder-bolts! The glare
> Of lightnings burned the sulphurous air!
> Not idle bolts of mythic Jove,
> But God's own answer from above.
> I woke—hill, valley, prairie, flood,
> One sea of blood! One sea of blood!
> It stained the land, the sea, the sky;
> O, God of peace! O, God of war!
> I knew what for! I knew what for!
>
> One dead in every house! O, land,
> Planted and dressed by God's own hand!
> O, sons of heroes, snatched to heaven
> In lightning-chariots, angel-driven!
> O, statesmen, clad in trust divine,
> Read! read! O, read the awful sign!
> The Slave! Aye, brother of our blood,
> Offspring, heir, image once of God!
> Soul, flesh like His who died to save—
> It is the Slave! It is the Slave!"

Perhaps it may be attributed to our weakness, more than anything else, that in the enjoyment of any great and costly blessing, we so often lose sight of what the blessing cost—the price that was paid for it. I know the principle is true with us, in regard to the greatest gift God ever made to man—I mean the gift of his Son. We live in the enjoyment of this great gift from day to day, but seldom pause to count the cost! Count the cost! did I say. Aye, who is *able* to do this? Who among all the sons of earth, or angels in heaven, is able to tell what is implied in the sublime truth, that *He* who expired on the cross, in the person of the Son of God, was our brother; that the blood shed there was fraternal blood. As members of a sinful family, we do well to follow the example of the Mary's in the gospel, and often prepare spices, and ointments, and as often go in *faith* to the grave of our Lord. It will do us good; it will help us to remember the price of our blessings. With all reverence I would make the application. God has given us a great country. The sun shines on no greater. It is great in its resources, it is great in its dimensions, and it has a great history. A history written in blood. We have been preserved, by the goodness and power of the Almighty, whose hand-writing may be seen on every page of our history. For—

> " Soon as the nation's heart was broke,
> God stayed at once the avenging stroke,
> And smote for us, with his rod,
> For man is man when God is God."

I believe, if we may judge of the future by the past, that we have a great destiny—a great future. The war-cloud has lifted, and the future smiles. Now, if we would be true to ourselves, true to humanity and true to God, we must not forget the price we paid, and the mercy of God, in preserving for us an undivided country, with its civil, political, and religious liberties. I fear there is danger in this direction. If we shall become intoxicated with our national glory, and the great achievements in science that we are making, and forget God, humanity, God may yet disown us, and our sun which now shines so brightly, may set in an endless night. As a preventive of this, I regard a proper observance of the pleasing, and at the same time, painful duty and task you have assembled to perform. The grave is a fit place for meditation. To-day we may think of the past, and contemplate the future. The occasion suggests sadness and mourning—a grief not unmingled with hope and joy, based upon a full belief that your comrades suffered and died to preserve and perpetuate *freedom, civilization, and Christianity.* All honor, then, to the noble sons and fathers whose lives were freely given as the price of our liberties. Here come, friends and soldiers, and weave your chaplets of flowers, and bring your evergreen sprigs, and strew the beauties of nature upon the graves of your fallen comrades. You can well afford to do this; *they* fought to win a crown, that *you* live to wear. The flowers you bring are a fit emblem, not of war, strife and bloodshed, but of the peace and union they fought to secure. The flowers will soon fade and die, and are also emblematical of the glory of man and the warrior's ambition. But your evergreen sprigs speak of man's immortality, and the fame of the true warrior. For,

> " When all the blandishments of life are gone,
> The coward sinks to death, the brave live on!"

At the close of these remarks, the soldiers proceeded, with open ranks, by each soldier's grave, and placing a wreath upon the same, each man deposited his portion of flowers. This simple, yet touching tribute, seemed beautiful, and yet mournful—and as they marched from grave to grave, the band discoursing its sad and mournful dirge, every eye watched their footsteps; and it seemed that it was but yesterday that we laid away those brave sons and fathers, who so nobly served their country in the hour of peril and darkness.

From this place they proceeded to the old cemetery, where they were addressed by the Hon. E. M. Plimpton, a member of the Post, who spoke briefly, and in an appropriate manner. At the close of his address, the same sad and pensive music filled the air—the same slow, measured tread of the soldiers, as they marched from grave to grave, depositing their garlands on the last resting places of their dead comrades. True, some looked on with idle curiosity, and others with an air of indifference; but the mass seemed to enter into the spirit of the occasion, and quiet and good order was universal. Some, also, as the soldiers marched away, lingered, perhaps to drop a tear on the grave of a loved one, and gathering from the tokens left by them, a small testimonial, wended their way, sorrowing, but with this recollection—*They were* TRUE *to their country.*

One feature that added greatly to the occasion, was the appearance presented by the soldiers, in their neat and tasteful uniforms, which added greatly to the interest of the ceremonies.

CHARLOTTE.

The members of Post Clark, Charlotte, Mich., performed the beautiful ceremony of strewing the graves of soldiers with flowers, on Sunday, May 30th. Notwithstanding the rain, a number of citizens accompanied the procession to the Cemetery. Each grave was visited, and each hero was remembered with tributes of affection and gratitude. They then adjourned to Sampson Hall, where the meeting was opened with prayer by Rev. B. F. Bradford, which was followed by an appropriate address, of which we give the following:

EXTRACT FROM ADDRESS OF ED. W. BARBER.

Members of the Grand Army of the Republic:

Let me say to you that you cannot pay a lovlier tribute to the memory of your departed comrades, than by meeting annually to strew flowers over their graves. A more beautiful memorial service could not have been devised. The tie that binds you to your comrades has been rendered sacred by their death. Let the years be many before you neglect this appropriate custom. I envy you the right you have acquired to pay them this tribute —so simple, so beautiful, so affecting. Without pomp or display—without music, if need be, save the requiem chanted by the sighing trees as they bend above your dead companions—we bid you come each year and revive your love of country and of liberty, as you cast upon their ashes the violet, the rose, the lily, and all the wealth of spring's choicest treasures. Willingly we heard your summons to join in the public ceremonies to-day. But words are incapable of a pathos so sweet as the incense of the flowers you have brought to deck the graves of our soldier-dead.

As long as you shall keep up these services, you will not be alone in observing them. You were not alone to-day as you assembled around the graves. It may be that from the bending heavens your comrades, though invisible to mortal eyes, filled your minds with generous thoughts and your hearts with holy emotions. But, however this may be with you, as now, the wife will come again and again to place a cross of flowers over a husband's grave. With you, as now, will come the aged father, and the tear will follow down the furrow Time has plowed upon his cheek, as he calls to mind the image of the soldier-boy sleeping at his feet. With you, as now, will come the mother, tenderly cherishing the memory of her son, as she places a flowery emblem of her affection upon the spot where he sleeps the sleep that knows no waking, her motherly grief consoled by the thought that he died a hero. With you, as now, will come brothers and sisters, and loving friends, each bearing some blossomed token of affection to the City of the Dead. And with you, as now, will come the orphaned ones, seeking their father's grave, yet proud in their sorrow to know that he died for his country.

But, some one might ask, why keep up these sad observances? Why keep alive the remembrance of the terrible conflict which required so many precious lives before the demon of war could be stayed? Because, I answer, of the lesson it teaches us—*that the pathway of justice is the only pathway of peace!* Because it teaches us that national crimes cannot escape punishment; and when a national evil becomes so glaring and defiant that only the red plowshare can uproot it, then war comes, springing from the hydra-headed evil itself, to scourge or to destroy.

Aye! we need to be reminded while pursuing the ambitions of the hour, or reaching out our hands graspingly for gain, that these men died for their country, and in dying gave all they had, to its cause. We need to be reminded, as the dread lesson written in blood does remind us, that in order to have peace and preserve it, we must, in our national capacity, respect, protect and defend the rights and liberties of the poorest man and the humblest, as well as of the richest and the proudest. And, above all, we need to be reminded that no nation can tolerate any form of slavery or oppression with impunity, and hope to escape the avenging hand of retributive justice.

Remembering all these things, and governing our acts as citizens, accordingly, we shall do well. And we cannot forget them, if we come with each recurring year to refresh our memories by the side of the flower-strewn graves of our soldier-dead.

Then, when we ask ourselves the question: Why did these men die? the answer will come unbidden: Because the hour for the final conflict between Freedom and Slavery—irreconcilable here as everywhere—upon this continent had come, and whether knowing it or not, every soldier, sleeping his last sleep or among the living to-day, was an instrument in the hands of an overruling Providence to wipe out the guilty stain of a nation's sin.

Beautiful as are the tributes this day paid, a better service than is found in flowers, dirge or oration, shall we render their memories by emulating the spirit and carrying on the work they so nobly commenced. Our fathers by their heroic deeds, gave existence to our nation. Their sons and descendants, with an equal valor, have defended the principles they established, and have given freedom to every person within the national limits. And now the great duty devolving upon us is to persevere until the last battle in behalf of equal rights and equal laws for all shall be fought and won, and equal privileges under the law be irreversibly secured as the birthright of every American citizen. Let the ceremonies of this day be perpetuated until that glad time shall come.

When the nation shall be lifted to that proud eminence, the Genius of America, engraved in enduring marble, may be placed between the statues of Liberty and Justice, in the national temple, there to remain forever. With these twin principles for its support, and the strong hands and brave hearts of the millions who are to people this country ready to rally for its defense when assailed, we have a sure and permanent guarantee for peace. Peace is what the nation needs. It wants no more war. It should have no more unless compelled to wage it in defense of its cherished principles.

With our present magnificent domains stretching from ocean to ocean, and from the orange-groves of Florida to the ice-fields of Alaska, war for the acquisition of territory, or to gratify a lust for dominion, would be a monstrous crime. Bunker-Hill and Yorktown, Lundy's Lane and New Orleans, Fort Sumpter and Appomattox, with all the scenes of blood and carnage associated with these historic names, furnish war pictures enough to satisfy the most sanguinary imagination for a century. He is a bad statesman, and proves that he has become oblivious to the highest interests of his country, who threatens war to settle any international dispute, the importance of which is measured by a computation in dollars and cents. For the triumphs of peace are greater, and surer, and nobler, than the highest possible achievements upon the field of battle.

War is only justifiable when waged in defense or for the preservation of human rights. When a despotism has become so rank and oppressive as to be no longer tolerable—or when despotic elements have banded together, as in our recent struggle, to tear down the temple of liberty and to substitute in its place a charnel house of oppression—it is the right, it is the duty of a people to use all the means God and nature have placed at their disposal to crush the oppressor, and to prevent the foul wrong from being consummated.

It is when the contest is of this nature that it affords the deepest interest to the patriotic heart. Then the lover of liberty awaits the result, with pale cheek and suspended respiration. Not, however, because he hates war the less, but because he loves liberty the more. Hence, in our mighty struggle, the painful anxiety that filled every loyal breast. It was because upon the issue hung suspended the fate of our beloved country. If victory perched upon the standard of the Union, our homes, our altars, our firesides were safe, and liberty was secure in its last chosen place of refuge forever. The grandeur, then, which gathers about this war for the Union, is aside from and above all its battle scenes, though the continent shook beneath the tread of a million armed men engaged in the bloody arena. For not the destiny of one nation, or the hopes of one people only, were involved in it. It cast its influence not upon one age only; but the destiny of the world, the cause of mankind, the interests of future generations, were all enlisted on the side of the Union.

From first to last we had the cordial sympathy and moral support of the patriots of every land, who are waiting and hoping for a deliverance from the despotisms that surround them; while, on the other hand, the rulers of nearly every monarchy on the globe gave undoubted evidence of sympathy with those who sought the nation's destruction. Why was this? It is because the monarchs fear the example of a great, powerful, free Republic. It is because this country is regarded as the last refuge of Freedom; its only hope and home upon the whole earth. For these reasons the eyes of the world were turned towards us, watching with the intensest interest, the varying fortune of the war for the preservation of our liberty and nationality.

And now the friends of men in every nation look to us with anxious hope, and implore us to be faithful to our great trust; the memory of the great and good of all ages supplicates us; the noble army of martyrs in the cause of humanity stretch out their hands to us; the blood and the sacrifices of our fathers beseech us; the yet undimmed recollection of three hundred thousand patriot graves appeals to us; the innumerable throng among the angel hosts, who have passed from Freedom's battle-fields on earth to the perfect freedom of the heavenly state, look down upon us from the holy heights they occupy and plead with us;—all, all, entreat us, by whatever makes life desirable and the heart holds dear, to preserve the spirit of Liberty. We are admonished by the wrecks of nations that lie scattered along the shore of time; by the ashes of dead Empires, that

perished because of their oppressions of the children of men
—by all that has been suffered and endured in the great cause
of individual freedom—not to forsake it or let it suffer while
entrusted to our keeping.

In the unity of the Republic, to preserve which the very elect
of the land lie sleeping in honored graves, with equal laws and
equal privileges for all, is to be found the only certain guarantee for peace, prosperity, and happiness. National safety,
national tranquility and national glory, all require that the
national law shall be based upon the fundamental principles of
Eternal Justice.

We have a glorious country. It is a cause for daily gratitude to the Giver of all Good that our lot has been cast under
the care of so beneficent a government. Let no dream of dis-
ruption or destruction enter the mind of any American citizen
to be harbored for a single moment. Cicero has attributed the
decline and fall of the Roman Empire to a forgetfulness, on
the part of her people, of the principles they had recognized
in their earlier and happier fortunes.

Let us not forget the foundation idea of our government, as
embodied in that immortal rescript of human rights—the Dec-
laration of Independence—and cease to cherish and protect
the inalienable rights of man. If the Republic remains true
to this idea, its example will not be like that of other Republics which have dotted the world's history, affording another
unhappy instance of the failure of institutions intended to
provide for the protection of human liberty.

How sad is their history—how impressive the lessons they
teach—how mournful the wrecks they have left.

> " Such is the moral of all earthly tales ;
> 'Tis but the same rehearsal of the past.
> First freedom, and then glory : when that fails,
> Corruption, slavery, barbarism at last ;
> And history, with all her volumes vast,
> Hath but one page."

A country that is worth dying for as men have died for this
—a country that is worth suffering for as men have suffered

for this—is worth preserving by a rigid adherence, on the part of every citizen, to the great idea of personal liberty, wherever it rests. This preserved, its peace is rendered secure and its prosperity certain. God grant that in the future there may be given no occasion for a repetition of scenes like this.

War brings blighted fields, desolated homes, and saddened hearts. Peace brings nobler trophies in ripened harvests, happy firesides, and joyous hearts. The grandest triumphs of the people of this country are not to be found in the cannon they have invented, in the Monitors they have built, in the dread machinery they have produced for destroying human life. Not to these things do we point with the proudest enthusiasm, as the great achievements of American civilization.

Our greatest, noblest, and proudest triumphs have been won while following the white-robed angel of Peace. Here the inventive genius of man is as free as the institutions under which he lives; and we point with the greatest delight to the wonderful achievements it has wrought; to the Steamer, which laughs defiance at wind and tide as it rides the ocean's breast; to the tamed lightning, which, by means of the telegraph, ministers to the necessities and aids the enterprise of man; to the coil of wire which rests upon the ocean's bed and makes the Old World and the New feel the same electric touch, and furnishes a new guarantee for peace; to the iron rails that stretch across the continent, so that, passing through the golden gate of California, we are nearer the ancient civilizations of the East than are the monarchies of Europe—enabling the Occident and the Orient to shake hands across the broad sea that should ever remain Pacific; to the school-houses that are dotted over every township; to the church spires that point heavenward from every city and hamlet as the emblems of our Christian civilization.

Such are the triumphs of Peace. Said I not well, then, that they are higher, nobler, and grander than all the battle-fields of the world? Oh, then, for the future, in the language of the

Commander-in-Chief of the armies of the Republic—"Let us
have peace."

> " Lord of the Universe! shield us and guide us.
> Trusting Thee always, through shadow and sun,
> Thou hast united us, who shall divide us?
> Keep us, O, keep us, the MANY IN ONE!
> Up with our banner bright,
> Sprinkled with starry light,
> Spread its fair emblems from mountain to shore;
> While through the sounding sky
> Loud rings the nation's cry—
> UNION AND LIBERTY! ONE EVERMORE!"

COLDWATER.

The ceremonies which took place in this city on Saturday,
May 29th, under the direction of Post No. 34, G. A. R., Capt.
J. H. McGowan commanding, were attended by several thousand of the people of Coldwater and vicinity. Although the
rain fell in torrents, over 200 conveyances formed in the procession, which, together with the large number on foot, including the Masonic Fraternity, the Good Templars and Grand
Army of the Republic, moved to Oak Grove Cemetery, where
the exercises were to have taken place. Near the entrance to
the grounds a large cenotaph had been erected, in memory of
the deceased soldiers buried elsewhere. Owing to the drench-
ing rain, Commander McGowan announced that the oration and
addresses would be deferred until the afternoon.

The committee of little girls, 150 in number, dressed in white
with red belts and blue sashes, then visited the grave of each
soldier and scattered flowers and wreaths upon their resting
places, Commander McGowan announcing the name and age
of each, and the command to which he belonged, the Cornet
band playing a dirge meantime, when the procession broke up,
and all sought shelter from the still falling rain.

The rain ceasing about three o'clock, it was decided to have
the addresses in the Court House yard, and a large crowd
assembled and listened to the following

63

ORATION OF CAPT. G. H. TURNER.

Worthy Commander, Fellow-Soldiers and Citizens:

In the peculiar fitness of things, it seems some more eloquent tribute than mine, graced by maturer years and the added weight of riper experience, should solemnize the mournful duty that we render this day to our honored Dead.

But these silent sleepers need no word-painting or pen-pictures to eulogize their actions in our struggle for national existence. The eloquent silence above these little mounds is plainly suggestive of that devotion to duty, that self-sacrificing spirit, that patriotic enthusiasm that characterized our loyal soldiery.

Roll back but a few years the resistless course of time, and how the scene changes. Peace, with the seductive security of continued prosperity showered blessings upon us as a nation. Our fields teemed with an abundant harvest, our barns were bursting with plenty, our rivers were dotted with the white sails of commerce, and no nation so distant or so powerful but what did reverence to the stars and stripes. Like the everlasting mountains that resist the external war of elements and only crumble by the internal throes of that gigantic Titan imprisoned in their bosom, so we stood, unapproached by external foes, but nourished a deadly Upas in our own breast. The shadows of this poisonous tree had so gradually stolen upon us, that by very familiarity we had overlooked its fatality, when, lo! the cry comes from Washington that sacrilegious hands are tugging at the heart of the nation and strong arms and brave hearts must help, in this hour of need, or we perish. This appeal came individually to every loyal heart, and most glorious was the response. Soon we saw the streets of our city, whose quiet had only been disturbed by the peaceful ways of trade, resounding to the marching squadron, or shaken by the reverberating echoes of our artillery. Grim-visaged war usurped the field where agriculture brought her yearly tribute in ripened grain and luscious fruits. Flora, Ceres, Pales, fled

at the approach of Mars. Ah! those were days that com-
pressed years of anxiety in moments of time. How indelibly
the scene is impressed upon the mind and heart that transpired
when the first Company, under the patriot hero, Capt. Eb.
Butterworth, mustered at the depot for departure. The joyous
laugh of infancy was checked by the saddened countenances of
older people, and the more matured in years that realized the
situation felt the awful responsibility of the hour, while old
age with faltering steps came with trembling lips to utter God
speed. And, when the last words had to be spoken, and the
last lingering clasp of affection loosened, how impenetrably
dark seemed the cloud that hung over us, whose sombre folds
were only pierced by that Divine light which the Angel of Mercy
flung down through the gloom. How we listened for the familiar voice, or strained the ear to catch the distant foot-fall, and
how unconsciously the eyes wandered in the direction they
departed. Something had gone out of our lives, and though
hope unrolled the silver lining of the cloud to our view, anxiety
laid bare each dread possibility. Yet for four long years these
partings were transpiring in our midst, partings whose sundered
chords should not be re-united this side of eternity, until a wail
of anguish ascended to Heaven in piteous accents—how long,
oh! Lord, how long!

This is but a reflection of what was transpiring through all
the loyal States. How grand is that consciousness of manhood that takes upon itself the burden of duty and pursues
undeviatingly the moral promptings of the heart, though sacrifices are strewn by the way-side, and self-aggrandizement is
absorbed in mutual disinterestedness. Our soldiers needed not
the exhortation that Napoleon found necessary to utter to his
troops, when he stood beneath the Pyramids and exclaimed,
"The suns of forty centuries are looking down upon you!"
No, in every loyal heart there was a knowledge of the responsibility that rested upon each one, and a glow of honest pride
that animated every countenance when they remembered their
efforts were helping to perpetuate that government which bears

this motto on its bright escutcheon—*"Salus populi suprema lex esto."*

We will never again have to search ancient history for an example of the Grecian mother, who, in presenting her son with his shield as he went forth to battle, told him to come with it or on it. She has at last found her equal in heroism in the daughters of America. With the loving hands of wife, mother, or sister, you assisted in the preparation of departure to the scene of battle, those near and dear to you as your own life; and though every action on your part seemed but the knell to that saddest of all words—farewell—no sigh escaped you. Womanly devotion rose to the majesty of martyrdom, and you proved yourselves loyal, brave, and true. Though you sent your friends to meet the foe in deadly strife, they went in all the pride, pomp, and circumstance of glorious war, surrounded by enthusiastic comrades, cheered with the hope of some crowning victory, enlivened by strains of martial music, and soothed by the knowledge that all at home were well, and, above all, that that starry flag should wave in all the purity of its simplicity over this land of the free and home of the brave. On the contrary, you were tortured by anxiety and suspense, breaking the seal of every letter with trembling hands, lest it confirm your fears, and with suspended breath scanning the long list of names reported missing, wounded, or dead, but with the devotion of American womanhood, moved on, worked on, loved on.

It is not necessary for me to designate by name the heroes that sleep here around us. Their eulogy is blazoned as bright as the flashes of their musketry in the scarred and jagged sides of Mission Ridge, and the frowning battlements of Lookout Mountain. Time will not dim its lustre, and like a coronet of gems set above the world, will be to our children's children the sacred emblem of National glory. They have chronicled their deeds on the field of Antietam and Gettsyburg, from the Atlantic to the Pacific, from the Ohio to the Gulf of Mexico. Their

history is written in the hearts of their countrymen, and
though marble piles shall rise in commemoration of their
deeds, let the story of their life and death descend as national
history from generation to generation, and still live in future
ages when the marble tablets shall be crumbled into dust.

Soldiers, rest! Your warfare's o'er;
Sleep the sleep that knows no waking;
Dream of battle-fields no more,
Days of toil and nights of waking.

In commemorating these graves, do not let us forget the
nameless ones scooped from the blood-stained field of battle,
or hollowed by the way-side too hastily to admit a comrade to
mark his last resting place, save in memory. May Nature, in
sympathy with her darling dead, rear sweet spring flowers over
those graves, whose blossoms, though born to blush unseen,
shall not waste their sweetness on the desert air. And those
marines who sleep beneath the waters they so heroically defended, let the full share of honor be meted to them. Though
watching with sleepless fidelity the long line of our coast, or
sending broadside upon broadside into the very teeth of the
rebel forts, they never, for a single instant, disgraced the flag
that floated at the mast-head, but gave to our fleet her proud
eminence among the navies of the world. One could multiply
instances of their valor, like the brave Cushing, that destroyed
the Albemarle, or when Commodore Farragut attacked the
rebel fleet under the very walls of Fort Jackson and St. Phil-
lip. Though three hundred guns rained their destruction of
shot and shell upon him, he and his brave command carried
his vessels through that baptism of fire and blood till the
Crescent City crowned his victory. It was a sad Saturday for
us when the Merrimac steamed from her hiding place, and
headed direct for our shipping that guarded Newport News.
The Congress and Cumberland poured broadsides of solid shot
upon the mailed sides of the monster, but disdaining even a
reply to the iron hail that bounded from her sides, she buried
her prow, with a fearful crash, into the side of the Cumberland

and dealt her a mortal wound. Recoiling from the shock, she poured a volley into the already sinking ship; but Lieutenant Morris and his command preferred to sink with his vessel than to surrender to the enemies of the old flag. Slowly the Cumberland was submerged, but continued hurling defiance at the rebel monster, and her last moan was a broadside as the waters closed over her. When I saw the tall spars of his vessel still piercing the blue waves, they seemed to me like the finger of destiny pointing to the God of Battles, and while the James shall roll its waters to the sea, let a grateful nation honor these heroic men.

The grave of every hero before us covered by the green mantle that Mother-earth folds so lovingly around them, has a corresponding grave in some heart where the flowers of memory bloom, nourished by that fountain of affection whose waters spring from eternal hope. The sable habiliments of mourning, speak of these deeds a language that cannot be mistaken, and we come to-day to render tributary honors to those who have gone before; to extend the hand of mutual sympathy; to mingle our tears with you; for your sorrows are our sorrows. The eloquent interpretation of the silence of the sepulcher tells plainer than words; they were found in the line of their duty *at the front!* We who have lived to enjoy their labors, whatever else occurs to us, their place in our memory should be *at the front.* They have passed beyond the reach of mortal aid and sympathy, but they have left behind them a legacy which should be a pleasurable duty to us to assist in every possible way. We can show our devotion to the dead by doing our duty to the living. The orphan, the widow, and the afflicted should be our special care. We owe them a debt of gratitude which we can never repay, but we can in a measure relieve their necessities, not only with words of condolence, but hasten in a pecuniary way to lighten the burdens of life. Let them not feel they are recipients of charity, for we are their debtors, and we should be profoundly thankful that so small a remuneration on our part could be placed in the balance of the awful

contribution they have made. Let the consecrated places of
our honored dead be held in reverential awe and profound
regard as the sacred deposits of the nation's defenders; for, in
that great day when the sky shall pass away as a scroll, the
fountains of the deep be broken up, and the graves give up
their dead, the marble cerements of Notre Dame, or the sculp-
tured Sarcophagii of the ancient Pyramids, will yield no more
sublime example of patriotism than the quiet and unostenta-
tious graves around us. Let fragrant flowers rest over each
loyal heart, emblems of peace, purity, and love, and when the
snow-white flag of Jesus shall be the universal banner of the
world, their fragrance shall rise as incense to the angel of
Mercy who will send greeting to us, "Peace on earth and good
will to man."

ADDRESS BY REV. W. C. PORTER.

Fellow Citizens:

I but speak the language of your own hearts when I say,
beautifully appropriate have been the ceremonies of this hour,
as with reverent hearts the hands of youth and beauty have
strewed the offerings of peace above the sacrifices of war.
Beautiful the ceremony certainly is, as in this quiet "city of
the dead," old and young unite in doing honor to the memory
of those who gave their *all* to the cause which they and we
regarded as the cause of their country and of humanity, and
above their graves strew chaplets and garlands of those spring
blossoms with which the loving Father of all hides the ravages
of winter. Over the ravages of winter, the channels worn by
the torrents and the seams cut by the ice, God sows the grace-
ful grasses and the modest violet. Convulsions and catastro-
phies, wounds, diseases and death, are one side of the picture
presented by all we know of life. But somehow we gain the
impression that this is not normal; for no sooner do we grow
sad at the sight of disaster, than we are cheered again by the
sights and sounds of ministering love. Not "Victory," the
victory of force, "and then the typhus," but victory with all it

comprises of evil, and then loves healing touch. First the canopy of fire and smoke, in which the patriot breathes out his soul, and then the era of peace and then the reign of order: first, the desert with its drouth, its conflicts and uncertainty, then Pisgah with its glorious visions and the Land of Promise with its rest. Such is the divine order. And when under the reign of Peace, surrounded with all the material blessings which come in its train, we, the citizens of a proud free nation, whose territorial integrity has been preserved, and whose political status has been exalted in the view of all nations, by the heroism of men who have the "courage to fight and the manhood to die" for the land they love, meet to manifest our appreciation of their sacrifice, what can be more beautiful than to see all ages and all classes stand about their graves in reverence, while the hands of innocent maidens—the flowers of our hearts and of our homes—strew the soldier's grave with the sweet blossoms of our gardens and our fields. Surely the ceremony is appropriate, for we but imitate, as I have suggested, that which God does in nature, and our scattered flowers are but a feeble imitation in our Cemetery of what he is doing throughout the earth. Does God plant flowers on the soldier's grave? Pardon me if I answer from experience, and relate an incident that can never be forgotten while memory lasts. About one year after the "Battle of Chancellorville," while on our march to that terrible conflict known in our history as the "Battle of the Wilderness," we bivouaced on the old battlefield, and anxious once more to see particular spots fraught with a terrible, a tragic interest, I sought that part of the field where the tide of battle had rolled and surged with most deadly violence. There were still to be seen, scattered all around, sad relics of the fight, while here and there unsightly mounds told of the haste in which friends, or the carelessness with which foes had hidden away the remains of men once fired with heroic ardor and patriotic devotion. How vividly the whole scene was recalled! Again I heard the sharp rattle of the rifles and the heavy roar of artillery, the shrill call of the bugle and the shouts of the combatants; all that fierce, wild uproar which marks the progress of the battle! As the shades of night gathered above me and I was reminded that it was time to return to my regiment, I longed to bear with me some memento which in after days should speak of that terrible conflict. What should it be? Around me lay broken arms, pieces of swords and muskets, and bullets marked "U. S." and "C. S." What should I choose? All were repugnant, for each spoke of human sufferings and death; so I stooped and gathered from the earth which lightly covered the soldier sleeping unconscious of wounds and death, a white and a blue violet, emblems of God's love, who thus watched over the ashes of the dead though away in the tangled woodlands of the south, far from the homes of kindred and childhood, when weary watchers had waited for their coming until hearts had grown sick and hopes died away; when eyes that had grown dim with weeping could let fall no tear-drops upon the rude mound, God was watching over the sleeper's dust, and had planted the timid violet, while kind nature had dropped upon the ground her fruitful showers and her pearly dews, and I, a former comrade, in the gathering darkness and the solemn hush of that summer eve, stooped and—not without emotion—gathered the violets from the soldier's grave. Beautifully appropriate are our services, as we thus imitate the loving care of the Father in Heaven. But there is another sense in which these services are highly appropriate. They are the offering of gratitude to valor. We can never forget that to the patriotism of our volunteers we are indebted for a united country. To the sacrifices of our citizens, our brothers, sons and husbands, we owe it, that to-day we are not plunged into the wild vortex of anarchy, and witness on every hand the sad spectacle of "States dissevered, discordant and belligerent," renewing on this fair land the feudes and deadly conflicts which have marked with crime and blood the pages of European history. And to the memory of those by whose sacrifices we are thus blessed, we owe not only that legal recognition, which, as a government we have made in pensions and bounties, unprecedented for liberality in the annals of the world, but also all loving tokens which can tell to survivors that the people of a glorious nation can never forget their heroes; that around the " hearth and home," their deeds are remembered and their names cherished with the warmest affection, by a grateful people. It is from our homes we draw our proudest inspirations. It is *for* our homes we strike with the greatest force. It is the memories of home that strengthen the hearts of " citizen soldiers " to bear all the hardships of the camp, and the horrors of the battle.

> " When the tempests of war surge round us and rattle,
> When the stoutest of hearts would be fain to succumb,
> What is it that nerves the most timid to battle?
> The blessed remembrance of Hearth and of Home."

And may that day never dawn when the armies of America will need to be supplied by mercenaries who feel none of the inspiration which supported our fathers in their struggle to secure a nation, and our brothers in their sacrifices to preserve it. We all know the proud boast of England's poet which became the watch-word of the nation:

> " Britania needs no bulwarks, no towers along the steep,
> Her march is on the mountain-wave, her home is on the deep."

But have we not a prouder boast? Do not we say with a pride words cannot adequately express, that the bulwarks and defenses of our country are found, neither in towers of stone nor ships of oak or iron, but in the love of the millions of her brave sons whose best energies are given to her prosperity in peace, and who, when her life is jeopardized, stand forth a living wall, stronger than adamant, and stem a fate to turn aside the dagger aimed at her breast, though the point may pierce their own hearts. Sad and presageful will be the day, if it shall ever dawn, when America cannot point in proud confidence to her sons and say: " These are *my* defenders; bucklered with these brave hearts and strong arms I stand secure!" And so it is befitting, it is appropriate, that by every proper demonstration we should do honor to the memory of the dead, that we may thereby increase the love and devotion of the living. To-day, all over our broad land the people will gather about the graves of our fallen heroes, as at altars of sacrifice to rekindle the torch of patriotism which God grant may never be extinguished. Here we have strewed our offering of sweet flowers above the graves of those whom we proudly name "Our Defenders." Spirits of the departed, if from your spheres of being you look upon our actions, be pleased to accept this deed as no hollow form, but the true index of our faithful remembrance. Here we renew our vows of faithful service even unto death, for the institutions you loved, the country for which you died.

But I cannot, I would not forget that I stand before you as a minister of the "Gospel of Peace," whose daily prayer ascends to the Father of all, for the dawning of that better age when " The nations shall learn war no more," in the full faith, that however long delayed, the promised day will come when "The Might with the Right and the Truth shall be," and all questions between nations no less than between individuals shall be settled on the principles of equity, in the spirit of love. But it is evident that day has not yet dawned, the spirit of wrong and injustice is not yet cast out, and too much of a selfish disregard for justice rules in the councils of the nations. Already there are ominous portents, strange whisperings are abroad, and there is a dread of impending evil in many hearts which has not and perhaps cannot shape itself in words; but while we may not anticipate the future, here beside the graves of those who died to preserve the unity of our nation, do I not speak the common sentiment when I say, that should any hand be raised in wrath against the land we love, we will rally as of yore to the defense, and maintain her honor or die in the endeavor? We have no lust for war, no thirst for slaughter— from its dire form we shrink with loathing as from the enemy of our race; but to a people there are greater calamities than war—to a man there are evils more terrible than death. And so, while we have consecrated ourselves to the cause of our

country, let us lift up our hearts in all sincerity to Him who
rules in the councils of nations and of men, and humbly pray
for guidance, for protection, and for peace.

APOSTROPHE, BY DR. J. H. BEACH.

Rest thee, heroes! In the firmament of glory
  We can trace each spirit star.
The distant years shall hear the story
  Of thy sacrifice in war.

Rest thee, heroes! let our gifts of choicest flowers
  Show our reverence for thy dust,
Whilst in heaven's elysian bowers
  Thy eternal spirits rest.

Rest thee, heroes! What although our humble effort
  Nought of good to thee imparts—
These faint tributes to thy merit
  Strengthen virtue in *our* hearts.

Rest thee, heroes! Lo, we bring our simple offering
  Stript of every marring thorn,—
Thus we come, of nought remembering
  But those virtues which adorn.

Rest thee, heroes! for, by thee our flag exalted,
  Gains the homage of the earth ;
But for thee, its fame departed,
  It had been forever curs'd.

Rest thee, heroes! Zephyrs o'er this broad domain
  Bear the fragrance of our token,
Whilst, united, all thy country shouts thy fame,
  And praises for its bands unbroken.

At the close of these exercises the audience was dismissed
with a benediction by Rev. G. P. Schetky. On Sunday, May
30th, appropriate sermons were preached by Revs. W. C.
Porter, G. P. Schetky, E. Cooley, and A. W. Curtis.

The neighboring villages of Quincy, Union City, and Bron-
son also observed the day by appropriate ceremonies.

DETROIT.

As the 30th of May—the day fixed for the ceremony of decorating the graves of the Soldiers of the Republic—fell this year on Sunday, the Memorial Services were held in this city, as in many other places, on Saturday, May 29th. This was the second observance of the day in Detroit, and the unanimity with which the people joined in the observance shows that the ceremony has a significance which is generally appreciated and approved. The weather was not very propitious. The sky was murky and threatening, and the ground was soaked with the rains of the preceding day, yet the ceremony was performed in Elmwood Cemetery, in the presence of at least ten thousand people.

Long before the hour for the formation of the procession, the streets were lined with people, and the hum of business ceased. Stores were closed, and flags were drooped at half-mast. The people gathered in crowds on the corners of the streets, and for two miles at least they filled the sidewalks so completely that it was difficult to move. The original programme was carried out, as far as circumstances would permit.

MAYOR'S PROCLAMATION.

Believing it to be the sacred duty of ALL to pay a just tribute of respect to the memory of those brave men who so nobly fell and died on the battle-field for the maintenance of the Union, the city offices will be closed on Saturday afternoon, May 29th, 1869, and the National Flag will be hoisted at half-mast, upon the City Hall and other public buildings, during the day, which example the shipping and citizens are invited to follow; also, our merchants and others are respectfully requested to close their various places of business from 2 to 5 o'clock P. M., on said day, in order that all may be allowed to participate in the memorial services.

WILLIAM S. BOND,
Acting Mayor.

MAYOR'S OFFICE, Detroit, May 24th, 1869.

Chief Marshal James E. Pittman issued orders, assigning to duty as Assistant Marshals on that day, M. V. Borgman, W. H. Allen, William Tillman, B. Vernor, William Hall, William Parker, E. S. Leadbeater, G. W. LaPoint, Chas. M. Lum, J. B. R. Gravier, H. M. Duffield, and S. E. Pittman.

ORDER OF PROCESSION.

Metropolitan Police.
Chief Marshal.
Assistant Marshals Borgman, Duffield, Hull, Pittman, and Lum.

FIRST DIVISION.

Assistant Marshals LaPoint and Leadbeater.
First U. S. Inf. Band.
First Regiment U. S. Infantry.
Co. G, Fourth U. S. Artillery.
Officers and Crew of U. S. Revenue Steamer Fessenden.
Detroit Light Guard.
Scott Guard.
Sherman Zouaves.
Officers, Soldiers and Sailors of the late War.
Disabled Soldiers and Sailors in Carriages.

SECOND DIVISION.

Assistant Marshals Tillman, Vernor and Parker.
Committee of Arrangements.
President of the Day.
Orators of the Day.
The Officiating Clergy.
Maj. Gen. John Pope, U. S. A., Comanding Department of the Lakes, and Staff.
Brevet Maj. Genl. Buchanan, U. S. A., Commanding Post, and Staff.
Officers of the Army, Navy, and Revenue.
Governor of the State and Military Staff.
Officers of the State Military Department.
State Military Board.
Senators and Representatives in Congress, and U. S. Ministers.
Officers of the U. S. Courts.
Civil Officers of the United States.
Judges of the Supreme and other State Courts.
His Honor, the Mayor.

The President, the Common Council, and City Officers.
Members of the Board of Police Commissioners.
Members of the Board of Fire Commissioners.
Superintendent of the House of Correction.
The Clergy of Detroit.
Members of the Board of Education.
Members of the Detroit Board of Trade.

THIRD DIVISION.

Assistant Marshals E. J. Garfield, and J. B. R. Gravier.
Knights Templar Band.
The Order of Knights Templar.
Lafayette Benevolent Association.

FOURTH DIVISION.

Assistant Marshal Allen.
Detroit Light Guard Band.
German Workingmen's Aid Society.
Cigar Maker's Union.

FIFTH DIVISION.

Assistant Marshal G. A. Sheley.

Shortly after two o'clock P. M., the whole body began to move, the signal being given by the firing of a gun from the U. S Steamer Fessenden, Capt. Knapp commanding, which lay off the foot of Woodward avenue, and which fired minute guns while the procession was moving. Saving the immense number of vehicles gathered at the gates of the Cemetery, there was nothing to retard the progress of the procession to the stand, on the grounds. There was no pushing or jostling, but an evident, deep seated desire to take part in honoring the dead soldiers.

The entrance to Elmwood was beautifully and appropriately decorated. It was surmounted by a broad arch, flanked by two smaller ones. The whole was draped with the national colors, and wreathed with evergreens, and bore the inscription: "Honor the Dead," with the date. A spacious platform, capable of holding several hundred persons, had been erected in the ravine near the fountains and the stone bridge. The sides of the hills, which rose adjacent, formed an amphitheatre, from which the thousands assembled could see and hear what was going forward. The platform was decked with evergreens and flags, and upon it were seated those who took part in the exercises, the orator and poet, many veteran and crippled soldiers, distinguished officers of the United States, State and city governments, clergymen, members of the board of trade, and others. The scene from the platform was impressive. In every direction there was a sea of faces. The sky was overcast, and the thick dark foliage on the hill-side, cast a sombre shadow, which seemed to be reflected in the faces of those who listened to the services of the hour.

EXERCISES AT THE STAND.

1. Prayer, by Chaplain W. G. R. Mellen.
2. Music, by the Choir.
3. Memorial Ode, by D. Bethune Duffield.
4. Memorial Hymn, by the Choir.
5. Oration, by President E. B. Fairfield.
6. Anthem, by the Choir.
7. Benediction.

THE SERVICES.

Gen. Mark Flanigan presided, and briefly introduced the exercises, after which an impressive prayer was offered by the Rev. W. R. G. Mellen, pastor of the Unitarian Church of this city. The following chant, written for the occasion by D. B. Duffield, was then sung by a quartette, accompanied by an organ: .

> How holy is this place!
> 'Tis sacred as the very house of God,
> And as the gate of Heaven.
>
> Here rests the Hero's dust,
> That hallows into Liberty this sod,
> For which their lives were given.

Ever tread lightly here,
Where sleep in honor all our soldier dead,
From life in glory riven.

How holy is this place!
'Tis sacred as the very house of God,
Yea! as the gate of Heaven.

THE DIRGE.

The poet of the day, D. Bethune Duffield, was then introduced, and recited, in a clear and pleasant voice, the dirge written by himself:

Bring garlands, rosy garlands,
    And strew these grassy graves!
For Heroes here are sleeping,
Where Liberty stands weeping
    For the bravest of her braves!

Bring flowers, fragrant flowers
    From off Spring's dewy breast,
For those who, thro' the battle,
Pass'd down 'mid War's wild rattle,
    To the Soldier's glorious rest.

Bring amaranthine flowers
    From Fame's far-shining crest;
For Martyrs here lie crowded,
In the Nation's flag enshrouded,
    With its glory on each breast.

Bring music, plaintive music,
    And pour it on the air;
But check, oh! check the bugle's cry,
And hush the snare-drum's wild reply,
    Thro' these quiet aisles of prayer.

Bring tears and sobbing bosoms,
    And press them on each grave,
For widow'd wives and mothers
Bewail these soldier brothers,
    And a hallowed memory crave.

Bring laurel-woven garlands,
    And crown these mounds of love,
For the sword is now laid by;
The conqueror pass'd on high
    To his welcome far above.

Bring our Country's peerless banner,
    And dip it to the grave;
That the spirits here who sleep,
Once more in joy may leap,
    To the flag they died to save!

After the reading of the dirge, the whole audience joined in singing, to the tune of "America," a chorus appropriate for the occasion. The orator of the day, the Hon. E. B. Fairfield, of Hillsdale, was then introduced, and spoke as follows:

ORATION OF PRESIDENT E. B. FAIRFIELD.

Soldiers of the Republic:

I greet you to-day as the nation's defenders—as the honored survivors of a great war waged for the preservation of our glorious fatherland. You meet—not on the bloody field any more, to be stirred by sound of drum and fife to deeds of noble daring, which eloquence and song shall forever embalm in the hearts of your grateful countrymen; but you come to stand by the last resting place of the fallen braves, to remember their deeds of heroic patriotism, and to bestrew their graves with tears and with flowers. It is a mournful, yet delightful office which you perform this hour in memory of your comrades who stood with you in the thickest of the fight, but fell ere the shout of final victory had burst on the air.

Men die, but their deeds live after them. The lips of these sleeping heroes are dumb, but their works do follow them and speak for them more eloquently than any poor words of the living can possibly do. Yet, on such an occasion as this, it is meet that we should pay them the best tribute we may by recalling to mind those deeds which speak their own praise, and which only needs a simple rehearsal to stir our hearts to gratitude as we walk softly and lovingly among their tombs to-day.

And, first of all, these men died for their country. Whatever there is of patriotic self-sacrifice—whatever there is of honor and glory in such a death—belongs to them. "Tell our countrymen that we lie here, in obedience to our country's laws and our country's call," might be the appropriate epitaph of every one of them. And, if the old poet has it right when he says—

"Dulce et decorum est pro patria mor:,"
(Sweet and glorious is it for country to die,)

the death of these men had in it no element of bitterness. He lives too long who outlives his country's life. A man without a country is most emphatically and sadly a stranger on the earth.

These heroes fought and fell for their altars and their firesides. Whatever is dear in the word "fatherland," had been assailed by the fratricidal hands that were raised to smite down the banner that floats to-day from lake to gulf, and from sea to sea. They came to its rescue; they wrapt its proud folds around them; sanctified it anew with their precious blood, and left it behind them glorified as never before.

"O, thus be it ever, when Freemen shall stand
Between their loved homes and the war's desolation.
Blessed with victory and peace, may the heaven-rescued land
Praise the Power that hath made and preserved us a nation.
And the star-spangled banner in triumph shall wave
O'er the land of the free, and the home of the brave."

But more than this; they gave themselves a sacrifice to the cause of Constitutional Government in our own land not only, but in the whole world besides.

That was the cause that was on trial before the nations, and for the righteous verdict in the case, these men shed their blood. For the advancement and ultimate triumph of well-ordered civil government by the people, and for the people, they gave up their lives, a willing, yet costly sacrifice.

Our country owes them a debt of gratitude and honor, which she will never be able fully to pay. A part of that heavy debt is ours. For us these men bared their breasts to the shock of battle. They stood between us and the foe, receiving in their own bosoms the deadly shafts that were aimed at their country's life. They died in war, that we might live in peace.

The Union was assailed; and in this Union rested our best hopes as a Nation. If its strong bonds were broken, there remained for us only the dissevered fragments of a once glorious Republic. The doctrine of one great National Sovereignty is the doctrine of peace and power; the doctrine of thirty-four petty Sovereignties that of weakness and war. With one strong government for the protection of the loyal and the true and for the punishment of all who rebel and betray, we are at peace among ourselves, and competent to conquer a peace with all mankind.

One flag means dignity, stability, and harmony; forty flags mean littleness, fragility, discord, and blood. The hands that in yonder cemetery lie folded in death, bore up the one flag of our common Union, and bore it until it floated again from every battlement and from every ship's deck.

If there is anything of which we, as Americans, might justly be proud, it is of the theory of the American representative Republic, which gives to us one strong central government for the common defense and the general welfare—a government demanding respect at home and abroad; while smaller matters of local legislation are left to the respective States. Over the door-way of our proud temple might well be inscribed the first words, so full of significance, which are found written in the fundamental law:

" We, the people of the United States, in order to form a more perfect union, establish justice, insure domestic tranquility, provide for the common defense, promote the general welfare, and secure the blessings of liberty to ourselves and our posterity, do ordain and establish this constitution for the United States of America." In defense of this our heroes fell· Absolutism had heretofore boasted of its strength, its efficiency·

and its permanency. It had taunted popular Government with weakness and insecurity. "Do these feeble fanatics fortify themselves? Even that which they build, if a fox go up he shall break down the wall." Monarchies were strong, Republics were weak. This was their boast and their jeer. But it is no longer. The successful overthrow of our great rebellion has taught the crowned heads of the world that "we, the people," can make the stablest and mightiest Government that earth ever saw; that no other Government beneath the sun has within itself greater capacity for self-preservation than has been displayed by the American Republic. Our stone wall has not fallen, though a thousand jackals have gone up over it. We have rebuilt the wall that had been thrown down—have revived the stones out of the heaps of the rubbish, and set up the doors upon the gates. One-half of the people have wrought in the work whilst the other half of them have held the spear and the shield. With one hand they builded and with the other fought, and at the end of the appointed days—though somewhat more than the ninety—the whole wall was joined together unto the half thereof with more completeness and symmetry than ever before; and as the monarchies beyond the sea witnessed the great achievement, they were much cast down in their own eyes.

From the day that Johnson and Lee surrendered to Sherman and Grant, Europe knew this was the stablest power on the face of the earth! The proof of this is not to be questioned; it is mathematical demonstration itself; the proof of figures that cannot well deceive us. There is no more delicate and sensitive test of such questions, than is furnished by the gold thermometer. And following hard after the conquest of the rebellion came the assassination of the Chief Magistrate, an event which in any monarchy in Europe would have been marked by a most sudden and rapid fall of their public stocks in the markets of the world. But what of American bonds in London and Paris, Frankfort and Vienna?. They scarcely depreciated a penny to the pound!

Henceforward it will not be questioned that an intelligent people are competent to govern themselves, and to maintain a national integrity despite rebellion at home and neutrality proclamations away from home. From this time the words of Sir William Jones will have even wider acceptance than ever before:

" What constitutes a State?
  Not high-raised battlements or labored mound,
Thick wall or moated gate ;
  Not cities proud, with spires and turrets crowned.
Not bays and broad-armed ports
  Where, laughing at the storm, rich navies ride ;
Not starred and spangled courts,
  Where low-brow'd baseness wafts perfume to pride !
No !—men, high-minded men,
  Men who their duties know,
But know their rights, and, knowing, dare maintain,—
  Prevent the long-aimed blow,
And crush the tyrant while they rend the chain !
  These constitute a State."

It has been demonstrated that a large standing army is not necessary to the exigencies of popular government. When the time comes which calls for men and money, they shall not be wanting. Hosts of the bravest will rush to their country's defense in the hour of its peril. At the tap of the drum, hundreds in every town will spring to their feet, and, shouting, "Here am I, send me," will seize their guns and fly with alacrity to the scene of deadly strife.

A government whose bulwarks are made strong by the willing hearts and ready hands of its own loving sons—rejoicing ever to do and to die in its defense—such government may mock at its foes. The elements of power and endurance are in it. Talk of Imperialism, of a royal house-hold, and of a blooded and titled aristocracy on American soil! Such plants will never thrive here. One blast of a sweeping nor'wester would wither them to their roots' ends. Whoever would amuse himself by the culture of such exotics, must nurture them carefully in the hot-bed of his own fevered brain, and shut them out from the sunlight of American intelligence, and the bracing air of this free North. They would never bear transplanting. With only the sickliest growth in the nursery of these wild fanatics even; outside of that, they would encounter instant blasting and mildew. Liberty's strong tree flourishes here. It is indigenous to American soil. It thrives on the rocks of New England, and on the mountain tops of Pennsylvania and Tennessee. The winds which sweep across the Northern Lakes fan its lungs into the largeness of a vigorous life, so that even its leaves are for the healing of the Nation. It grows luxuriantly by the side of still waters in Michigan, and strikes its roots deep into the broad prairies of the Mississippi Valley. This is its home; but Imperialism is at best a miserable house-plant, and, thank Heaven, found in but few houses at that.

For no such wretched end did our heroes die. In their last will and testament, sealed with their blood, they have bequeathed to us, as their dying legacy, a Union, stronger, nobler, freer than ever. "The blood of the martyrs is the seed of the church." By the gift of these men, and such as these, we have henceforth a more homogeneous country and a grander and higher civilization.

The freedom-loving of all the nations stand to-day on the graves of our fallen heroes to do them the homage of grateful tears for the bright hopes that they have brought to desponding hearts, that yet there is a good time coming, when the blessing of constitutional government of the people, by the people, and for the people, shall be enjoyed wherever the sun shines over the face of the broad earth.

Still more; it was in the interest of justice and freedom that these men fought and fell. It is much that they stood for their country's defense against the assaults of rebel hordes, who lifted their murderous hands to destroy the best government that the world had ever seen. But these men did even better than that. The traitorous hands that were raised to pluck down the flag, had wrought in the base work of building a government whose corner-stone was to be the absolutest despotism known to man. Rebellion has sometimes been in the line of justice—sometimes in the line of human advancement and freedom. But this, for the overthrow of which these men gave up their lives, was in no such line. They had undertaken to move back the pointer on the dial of the world's progress, more than fifteen degrees. Their march was backwards to barbarism. But the Divine voice had uttered itself from on high: "Speak unto the children of Israel that they go forward!" And though it was through the Red Sea, the voice must be obeyed. Reform only recedes when, in God's book of doom, a nation's destiny is sealed—only when the hand-writing appears on the wall: "Mene, Mene Tekel, Upharsin—God hath numbered thy kingdom, and finished it. Thou art weighed in the scales and found wanting. Thy power is broken, and given to others."

These men wrought better than they thought. The stone which the builders rejected is become the head-stone of the corner; and it fell to their honored hands and yours to lift to its place on the summit, where it catches the first beams of the morning—reflects back again to the last departing ray of the evening, and attracts the gaze of every beholder.

There is no other word quite so glorious in human speech as that word Liberty—no other sentiment quite so inspiring to human hearts as that expressed by its silvery notes:

> "Go, let the cage, with grates of gold
> And pearly roof, the eagle hold ;
> Let dainty viands be his fare,
> And give the captive tenderest care.
> But say, in luxury's limits pent,
> Find you the king of birds content?
> No! Oft he'll sound the startling shriek,
> And dash the grates with angry beak.
> Precarious freedom's far more dear
> Than all the prison's pampering cheer.
> He longs to see his eyrie's seat—
>   Lone cliff on ocean's lonely shore,
> Whose bare old tops the tempests beat,
>   Around whose base the billows roar,
> Or rise through tempest shrouded air,
>   All thick and dark, with wild winds swelling,
> To brave the lightning's lurid glare,
>   Or talk with thunders in their dwelling."

Such is that proud bird whom we have appointed to hold in

his beak the streamer which symbolizes to the world our American Independence. He flies high—his sharp eye sees afar. Now he plants himself on the mountain summit; now he leaves behind him the murky cloud and bathes in the serener light above. Let our loved America be ever as free as this bird of the mountains, which we have chosen as our national emblem.

No need of any more of that humiliation. That stinging taunt of jealous despots is forever at an end. No more shall they be permitted to mock when our fear cometh. "They that take the sword shall perish with the sword." Slavery did it, and died in the unholy war which she had so audaciously begun. We are not of the mourners to drop a single tear over the grave of this enchanting sorceress. Liberty is the heaven-robed virgin whose hand we kiss; and she lives!—lives in perennial youth and beauty—lives to wear the robes of a true royalty, and with such a queenly grace that all the hosts of the struggling shout with enrapturing ecstacy, "Viva Liberte! viva l'America!" Before her gracious sceptre all bow with a ready homage, rejoicing that now her domain has extended, so that she reigns without a rival where the Ohio and the Mississippi sweep their majestic waters; reigns along the shores of the Tennessee and the Alabama, the Potomac and the Savannah equally as by the banks of the Connecticut and the Hudson, the Penobscot and the Alleghany. "This is the Lord's doing, and it is marvelous in our eyes." But to these palsied hands, over whose resting place you drop your flowers to-day, it was given to do the last carving upon this beautiful gate of our Liberty's proud temple.

You come with no revenge in your hearts, even toward those whom you met on the field of blood. To the penitent among them, you may say, as Joseph to his brethren—"Be not angry with yourselves; ye indeed meant it for evil, but God meant it for good." To those who would still plot to do again the evil of the past, in view of their powerlessness and madness, you may utter the Divine prayer,—"Father, forgive them, they know not what they do!"

My task for the hour is a brief one. It is soon done. A
delightsome task it is to rehearse the parts which our brave
boys were called to act in the great drama of our Nation's life.
When our Tree of Liberty had begun to wither, and dead and
dying branches presented to us on every side their unsightly
forms, these were the men to water its roots with their blood,
until it should revive into greenness and beauty and symmetry
again.

A legend has come to us of the early days of our revolutionary history, of a plot to blow up an arsenal situated in the
midst of a New England village. The enemy had in the early
night laid a train of powder to a distance of two miles away.
This train was discovered by a brave patriot upon the very
instant of its explosion, with only time to throw himself across
the track of the line of fire. To think it, was to do it. The
flashing flame was arrested by his body—the plot had failed; a
thousand lives were saved, though he had died to save them.
Such is the acknowledgment which we make to-day of the
uncanceled debt which we who live owe to those whose memories we honor by the sweet flowers which we scatter above
them.

And scarcely less beautiful than the gorgeous flowers, is the
bright banner which their living hands bore, and which yours
carry still. That banner I greet to-day! All hail to the
Nation's flag! Behold it!

> " When freedom from her mountain height
> Unfurled her standard to the air,
> She tore the azure robe of night
> And set the Stars of glory there.
>
> She mingled with its gorgeous dyes
> The milky baldric of the skies,
> And striped its pure celestial white
> With streakings of the morning light;
> Then from his mansion in the sun
> She called her eagle bearer down,
> And gave into his mighty hand
> The symbol of her chosen land.
>   *   *   *   *
>
> Flag of the free heart's hope and home!
> By angel hands to valor given :
> Thy stars have lit the welkin dome,
> And all thy hues were born in heaven.

Forever float that standard sheet !
  Where breathes the foe but falls before us,
With freedom's soil beneath our feet,
  And freedom's banner streaming o'er us?''

CLOSING CEREMONIES.

At the conclusion of the address, which was received with
that homage which deep feeling pays to eloquence under such
circumstances, the final ode, written by E. P. Nowell, was sung
by the audience to the tune of "Old Hundred."

The benediction was then pronounced by Chaplain Seage,
and the procession reformed for the purpose of marching in
the avenues adjacent to the plots of ground laid out for the
dead soldiers.

There are 73 buried in one spot, and there are also about 40
graves of soldiers in various parts of Elmwood. As the procession moved the band struck up a solemn dirge. Four
detachments, each composed of four boys and eight girls, then
moved from the stand in various courses, and scattered the
bouquets of flowers on the graves. Many of the floral orna-
ments were exquisite in taste and were elaborate. Some of the
monuments over prominent soldiers or officers were draped
with the national flag, or otherwise decked with beautiful sym-
bols of affection and regret.

Taken all in all, there could not have been a more feeling
tribute paid by a people, composed of all classes, than that of
Saturday. There was no disturbance or noise, all was hushed
and still in reverent honor of the dead. Nothing whatever
marred the scene at the cemetery, and the whole assemblage
quietly dispersed at the conclusion of the exercises, so soberly
and thoughtfully that it was impossible to think they had not
been in a measure purified by the contact with the honored dead.

One gentleman and lady came from Chicago to see the grave
of their son properly decorated; an old lady, more than sixty
years of age, came over 100 miles to see the grave of her son
decorated, and many others came from a distance to attend the
ceremonies, and all were much pleased at witnessing the loving
care of the memory of their sons and brothers exhibited by
their former comrades.

On Sunday, the 30th, appropriate Memorial Sermons were preached in nearly all the Protestant Churches of the city. The Germans decided to observe this day by appropriate ceremonies, on the ground that, being the 30th of May,—the day set apart as Memorial Day,—it was proper that it should be observed. The weather, however, interfered materially with their programme. Rain fell throughout the early part of the day, and was still falling at the hour named for the commencement of the exercises, rendering the proposed proceedings at the cemetery well nigh impracticable, and they were abandoned. So far as relates to the processsion and oration, the programme was carried out. The company assembled at one o'clock, at Turner's Hall, on Sherman street, near Russell, and the ·procession started at two. Lucker's band was in the advance, followed by the various societies in the order named, to wit: Freie Turners' Society; Concordia Society; members of German Working Men's Aid Society; Social Turn Verein Society. The route was up Russell street to Gratiot, down Gratiot to Monroe avenue, down the latter to Campus Martius, down Fort to First, down First to Jefferson avenue, thence up to Randolph, up Randolph to Croghan, up Croghan to Rivard, up Rivard to Clinton, up Clinton to Russell, and thence back to the Hall. The procession was under charge of the officers respectively of the several organizations, and was conducted in fine order. Next followed the oration, by Mr. L. Klemm, Professor in the German American Seminary, on Lafayette street. It was a fine effort, embodying a graphic view of the war from its first inception; the difficulties experienced by the Government at the outset; the sacrifices of the patriot heroes who rallied to the vindication of national sovereignty and unity; and closed with an eloquent tribute to the memory of those who laid down their lives for their country. After the oration, the choir of the Concordia Society sang the popular and spirited German song, "Fahneneid," or the "Oath to the Colors," which closed the exercises.

12

GIRARD.

Saturday afternoon, May 29th, '69, at the appointed hour, the people assembled at the M. E. Church in this village, and under the direction of the Marshal proceeded to the cemetery, on the west prairie, where several of the soldiers are buried. Prayer, singing, and decorating the graves completed the ceremonies there; then the procession moved to the other cemetery, and after marching to each grave and depositing flowers, they marched to the orchard belonging to J. C. Corbus, Esq., where they had appropriate singing, and an oration by Dr. Clizbe, in which he did credit not only to himself, but the soldiers who lost their lives for their country and are now sleeping where their graves will be annually decorated with the choicest of flowers. Rev. Mr. Ware then paid a fine tribute to the memory of those soldiers who fell and were buried far from home and friends.

The decorating committee consisted of twelve young ladies, and the ceremonies were conducted without any attempt at show or splendor, and the length of the procession gave evidence of the interest taken by the people of Girard on this memorial occasion.

At a meeting of the citizens held on June 2d, '69, for the purpose of making arrangements for the Memorial Service, the question of erecting a monument to the memory of our deceased soldiers arose, and the meeting proceeded to organize, what is to be known as the Girard Soldier's Monument Association. The following is a list of officers elected: Rev. Wm. H. Ware, President; S. E. Lawrence and Miss Rose VanBlarcum, Vice Presidents; Geo. A. Russell, Secretary; Miss Irene Smith, Assistant Secretary, and Miss Eliza Day, Treasurer.

A Board of Trustees were also appointed, and a committee to draft resolutions and by-laws for the Association. They are determined to raise funds and erect a monument before the next anniversary, on which will be inscribed the name, rank, company, and regiment of every soldier who died from Girard, whether buried here or elsewhere. There are thirty-four in all; twelve are buried here, and the rest are sleeping where they fell, on Southern soil.

GRAND RAPIDS.

On Sunday, May 30th, 1869, for the first time in this city, the beautiful rite of strewing with flowers the graves of those who lost their lives in the military service of the nation, was generally observed, as recommended by the Commander-in-Chief of the Grand Army of the Republic. Probably over three thousand people were present at the different Cemeteries, and witnessed or took part in the ceremonies. It is hard to make a correct estimate of the numbers, which, great as they were, would doubtless have been more than double had the day been pleasant. The utmost decorum was observed throughout the entire proceedings, which seemed in all respects to harmonize with the day and the occasion.

The morning was misty and damp, and at nine o'clock it commenced to rain, and until about noon the clouds "wept in tears of gentlest rain," and again in the afternoon a soaking shower of an hour or more in duration took place at the hour when ceremonies were in progress at three of the Cemeteries. The general and concluding exercises of the day in the Fulton street Cemetery at five o'clock P. M., were hardly concluded when a pouring rain scattered the grand assembly of people.

GREENWOOD CEMETERY.

The people on the west side of the river where the cemetery is situated, had held meetings and made ample arrangements for the beautiful rite in which they were to engage. The soldier's committee, consisting of Col. T. Foote, Adjutant E. O. Stevens, Capt. J. W. Williamson, Capt. Alexander Milmine, Lieut. A. Yates, Capt. E. F. Covell and Capt. James Robinson, met at Engine House No. 3, at one o'clock P. M., and accompanied by about twenty other soldiers, marched to the Cemetery, a distance of about two miles, quite a procession of citizens in carriages, going with them. Arrived there they found and covered with flowers the graves of seven soldiers. After this was done, a hymn was sung by Mr. H. G. Porter, Mr. Shattuck and Mr. Stephens, and then Rev. W. B. Sutherland led in a beautiful and appropriate prayer. At the conclusion of the prayer another hymn was sung by the trio of singers. The gathering was quite large, notwithstanding the very inauspicious character of the weather, and flowers were there in superabundance.

OAK HILL CEMETERY.

The following named members of the soldier's committee met at the National Hotel at two o'clock P. M., and proceeded in carriages to the Cemetery: Col. E. S. Pierce, Maj. M. D. Birge, Col. Van E. Young, Maj. F. J. Fairbrass, Capt. H. N. Moore, Capt. G. W. Remington, Col. H. E. Thompson and J. D. Dillenback. They were accompanied by Rev. L. J. Fletcher, and also by Mr. H. Dean, who was assistant sexton at the time most of the soldiers were buried, and knew the locality of their graves.

An abundance of beautiful flowers had been generously provided by the ladies, and every head-board was decorated with a wreath or bouquet, and the graves nearly covered with their floral offerings. A brisk shower commenced just as the committee arrived at the Cemetery, and, as it showed no signs of immediate abatement, after waiting for a few minutes, the Rev. Mr. Fletcher, in a brief, but most eloquent address, spoke of the occasion of the gathering and the purpose it ought to serve in stimulating our patriotism. As he commenced speaking, the flood-gates of heaven were opened and the rain poured down harder than at any other time during the day. But he kept on, and the little band around him, most of whom had faced the leaden shower of rebel bullets and endured years of exposure to sun and storm in campaigns against the rebellion, were electrified by his words—earnest, heartfelt, christian words —worthy of the assembly, the man, his sacred office and the solemn occasion. He alluded to the day, the holy Sabbath on which Christ, our Redeemer, rose from the dead, and said it was fitting on this day to visit the graves of those to whom we owe so much, and strew them with flowers, for, as Christ rose from the dead, we believe that for them also is a glorious immortality, and if it is permitted from spirits above to view what is done upon the earth, we might hope that they were looking down from heaven, approvingly, upon the action, and our motives. He said that the most potent agency to preserve national harmony was the fostering of a spirit of devotion to the flag of our country, and cherishing with love and gratitude the memory of its defenders who gave their lives that the nation might live. After the conclusion of his speech he led in a short and appropriate prayer, after which the committee placed the flowers on the graves. Sixty-five graves were decorated, and the head-boards of a large number of them bore the words "U. S. Soldiers, unknown." The record of these graves is said to be in existence somewhere, so that all of them may be identified. We sincerely hope that such is the case, and that it will be done. Some lady, the committee could not ascertain whom, had provided many beautiful wreaths and crosses "for the graves of the unknown soldiers," and they were placed accordingly.

There were two fine gravestones, and at the grave of Geo. J. S. Chesebro, a beautiful monument. Four graves of unknown soldiers were found in the "Potter's Field" and left bright with tokens of remembrance.

Notwithstanding the heavy rain, a number of ladies were present in carriages. Mr. N. L. Avery and wife, Mr. A. B. Judd and family, Silas Pierce, Esq., Judge Robinson and others, were there in the rain to honor the memory of the known and unknown soldiers.

After the exercises of the day were all concluded the committee of soldiers, whose names are given above, held a meeting at Major Birge's, when the following resolution was passed:

Resolved, That, not forgetting any who furnished flowers, we hereby express our sincere and especial thanks to the lady, unknown to us, who arranged and gave the beautiful wreaths and crosses of flowers for the graves of the unknown soldiers.

CATHOLIC CEMETERY.

The committee appointed by the soldiers, headed by Capt. Coffinberry, Chairman, proceeded to the Catholic cemetery at 3 o'clock P. M., and met but few ladies and gentlemen, owing to the unpropitious state of the weather. We learn that a larger number were assembled at St. Mary's Church, but were prevented from attending by the rain.

The ceremonies were commenced by a short speech by Capt. Coffinberry, followed by Col. N. A. Reed, Jr. Then the graves were fully decorated with flowers, during which ceremony all were uncovered, while Capt. Coffinberry ponounced the formula over the grave.

After this sad ceremony had been performed all came together in a central position, where Lt. Adolph Campau read the hymn written by J. D. Dillenback for the day, and Col. N. A. Reed, Jr., read the following:

DECORATION HYMN, MAY 30TH—By SAMUEL BURNHAM.

They rest from the conflict, their labor is ended,
  Their battles are fought and their victories gained;
Their spirits heroic to God have ascended,
  Their memory is left us with honor unstained.

Beneath the green sod their bodies are sleeping,
  Above them in beauty the dewy grass waves;
While comrades this day are sacredly keeping,
  And strewing with flowers their glorious graves.

We know that our flowers will wither and perish,
  Our flags, too, will droop in the still summer air;
But deep in our hearts their memory we'll cherish,
  With love that the passing years ne'er will impair.

To us is the weeping, while theirs is the glory ;
    From danger and duty they ne'er turned aside ;
Heroic their deeds and immortal their story,—
    They fought for their country, and conquering, died.

No longer they listen the tramp of the legions
    That steadily marched to the field of the dead ;
From East and from West, and from far distant regions,
    Resistless in numbers and firm in their tread.

No angel of death o'er the battle-field bending,
    With skeleton finger is pointing his prey ;
Our God heard the prayers of the nation ascending,
    And turned our dark midnight of horror to day.

O, God of our fathers, O, God of our nation,
    Their faith was unwavering, their trust was in Thee ;
Thou gav'st them the victory, to our land gave salvation,
    And smiled once again on the home of the free.

Yes, honor and glory for them are eternal,
    The nation they ransomed their memory will keep ;
Fame's flowers immortal will bloom ever vernal
    O'er the graves where our heroes in glory now sleep.

The exercise concluded by Lt. Adolph Campau leading in prayer according to the usages of the Church—5 Peters, 5 Aves, Lord's Prayer, Hail Mary, and The Requiem.

GENERAL EXERCISES AT FULTON STREET CEMETERY.

The general and concluding exercises of the day took place at this cemetery at 5 o'clock P. M. A procession of soldiers under command of Gen. W. P. Innes, preceded by the Valley City Brass Band discoursing solemn music, marched from Luce's Hall, where they made their rendezvous and were supplied with flowers, to the cemetery and formed in a hollow square surrounding the grave of Rev. Dr. Francis H. Cuming, who was Chaplain of the Third Michigan Infantry, and the thousands of people present gathered around them as thickly as they could stand. Inside the square were the clergy, the quartette club, and the speaker.

The following order of exercises was observed:

1. Dirge—Valley City Brass Band.
2. Prayer—Rev. J. P. Tustin, D. D.

Many hearts prayed with him, as with moving solemnity he besought the blessing of God on our nation, built up and preserved by the sacrifice of so many heroic lives.

3. Hymn—" The Evergreen Shore."

By a quartette club consisting of the following named lady and gentlemen: Mrs. Patten, Mr. D. R. Utley, Mr. J. G. Hostetter and Mr. Osgood.

4. Address by Col. Geo. Gray, 6th Mich. Cavalry.

The speaker stepped to the centre of the square and stood silent for a minute or two, as though overpowered by emotion. Then he began his discourse by describing the sacred ties of loving memory that bind us to the dead. The honor that we pay the memory of our own departed friends is not a duty, but the simple dictate of nature. Toward those whose graves we now cover with flowers those emotions are heightened by the knowledge that their lives were given for us. He spoke of the Sabbath morning in April, 1861, when the telegraph flashed over the land the news that traitors had fired on the flag of our country in Charleston Bay, and of the glorious uprising of loyal men who left their business, their homes and friends, and sprang to the defense of the Union at the first call. He pictured their noble deeds, and the fate that befel so many of them on the battle field, in hospitals, or, perchance, after they came home to die in the arms of their friends. In whatever way they died it was for their country. The address closed with a sublime appeal to the patriotism of our citizens to maintain unimpaired the dear bought liberties we enjoy.

5. An Original Hymn.

Written for the occasion by one of the soldiers present—published on the day previous by both the city papers, and 1,000 copies distributed on the programmes—was read by Rev. A. J. Eldred, and sung by the audience present, led by the quartette club.

6. Benediction—Rev. J. Morgan Smith.

At the close of the services, the soldiers started to march to all the graves previously marked with small flags, but when two had been visited, the rain made it advisable to separate, and send a detail to each grave, which was accordingly done. The number of graves, as ascertained by the committee, was twenty-three.

After the people left the grounds, and most of them had reached their homes, a beautiful rainbow spanned the eastern sky for several minutes just before sunset—a fitting close for a day of such ceremonies.

HASTINGS.

Sunday, May 30th, being the day set apart for paying a tribute of respect to the memory of the soldiers who fell in the great struggle for freedom in the war of the rebellion, a due observance of the occasion was had by the citizens of this place.

The hour of three in the afternoon had been designated as the time for assembling at the cemetery, but a drizzling rain that commenced a little after noon, delayed the proceedings for nearly an hour, the weather proving quite inauspicious for carrying out the programme. And yet there seemed a fitness in the falling rain, emblematic of the shedding of tears o'er the graves of our dead soldiers. It seemed as though the very heavens united in paying the last sad honors to the departed by bedewing the sod that shrouded them in their last resting place with the glittering drops of the genial shower. Most propitiously did the rain storm cease at about four o'clock, when quite a large concourse of our citizens wended their way to the silent repository of the dead.

The exercises were commenced by an appropriate prayer by the Rev. A. P. Moors, of the M. E. Church, after which an excellent and touching address was delivered by the Rev. T. L. Pillsbery, late Chaplain of the 21st Michigan Infantry.

13

The speaker held his audience in breathless silence while he discoursed upon the occasion that had brought us together, pointing out the benefits resulting to us as a nation by the self-sacrificing spirit that bore our starry flag from victory to victory, and traced the hand of Providence in the great struggle that crowned our arms with the success that insures us a permanent and abiding peace. In concluding, the speaker paid a beautiful tribute to the memory of the fallen brave who had laid their lives a sacrifice on their country's altar.

The brass band, stationed in the middle of the grounds, then played a suitable dirge, while scores of children strewed beautiful bouquets and wreaths of wild flowers o'er the graves of the noble dead, each grave being designated by small American flags floating at the head of the mound. A death-like silence marked the exercises of the hour, which was only broken by the plaintive notes of the solemn music, and the sobs of friends and relatives as they bent over the grassy mounds that marked the abode of a husband, a father, or a brother. Tears commingled with the rain-drops, and heart-felt sympathy went from breast to breast, as sighs were wafted on the breeze.

Old Hundred was then played by the band, and the audience were dismissed with the benediction.

The occasion was one of great interest, and will long be cherished in our memories.

HILLSDALE.

The ceremony of decorating the soldiers' graves, took place in this city on Saturday, May 29th. At an early hour the citizens of the city and surrounding country began to congregate at the Court House in large numbers, each bringing beautiful bouquets, woven from the choicest flowers of spring, to be strewn upon the graves of those gallant, heroic men, who, in the hour of their country's peril, when the pulsations of the national heart grew still in awful suspense, lest with the next breath the great experiment of human liberty throughout the world, in the overthrow and death of the American Republic, should be no more; forgot the ties of consanguinity, and laying aside the peaceful avocations of civil life, buckled on their armor and sallied forth to mingle in the stern realities of war, and fell a bleeding sacrifice upon the altar of their country, bequeathing in their deaths to the present and future generations of America, the rich legacy of civil and religious liberty. The procession formed at 9 o'clock A. M., in Court House yard, under the direction of Gen. C. J. Dickerson, Marshal of the Day, assisted by Capt. Wm. H. Tallman, and marched to the old Cemetery, to do honor to the soldiers buried there. On approaching the Cemetery, the Hillsdale City Band struck up a funeral dirge. After the graves had been decorated a piece of music was sung by the choir, with melodeon accompaniment, which was followed by a touching and pathetic supplication to the Divine Father, by Rev. Mr. Parker, of the M. E. Church, after which another piece of music was discoursed by the choir. The procession then marched back to the Court House, the band in the mean time rendering music appropriate to the occasion.

After resting a few minutes, the procession was reformed and took up its line of march for Oak Grove Cemetery, in which a much larger number of soldiers are buried than in the old Cemetery, the procession being a half or three-fourths of a mile in length. The approach here was the same as before, the band playing a funeral dirge. After the several graves had been decorated, a piece of music entitled "Decoration Day," composed expressly for the occasion, was sung by the choir, which was followed by an impressive prayer by Rev. R. Dunn, each word of which in its awful earnestness seemed to breathe of Divinity, and made one feel that though he stood surrounded by the silent habitations of the dead, yet he was in the presence of the Living God and of angels. The prayer was followed with music by the choir, at the close of which Capt. Albert Dickerman, orator of the day, took the stand and commenced speaking in a very clear and eloquent manner, but a thunder storm coming on he was obliged to desist after speaking but a few moments, and the crowd of participants in order to get out of the rain, took the quickest and most expeditious course to get back into the city.

Taking the occasion altogether, it was one of which every soldier and citizen may well be proud, as in point of numbers and devotion, it showed that the people of Hillsdale county have not, and will not forget the services of their gallant dead.

LANSING.

—

COMMEMORATION DAY.

MAY, 1869.

BY MISS HARRIET SMEAD.

A golden sky, a world of beauty,
Bright with blossoms and green with leaves,
We wandering 'mid its marvelous mazes,
Binding the blossoms in beautiful sheaves.

Deftly twining them into garlands;
Weaving them into rare bouquets:
Frail blossoms, pure as the prayers of cherubs,
With an incense sweeter than songs of praise.

Over the hills, with the sun descending,
Slowly we go to the home of the dead;
The angel of Peace above us bending,
Parteth the willow wherever we tread.

Over the hills to the silent city,
God He knoweth our hearts are true;
Around the graves of our heroes kneeling,
Heaven above and their dust below.

Our fallen soldiers, we kneel around them,
With reverent fingers we deck their tombs;
Drop by drop was their life-blood given,
To save unto us our precious homes.

Our country's honor, our country's banner,
Safe they bore through the blazing lines;
For them doth Liberty sing high anthems,
And their graves are a grateful nation's shrines.

For them the Heavens have heard our wailings,
For them the day beheld our tears ;
Theirs be the shrines for votive garlands
Forevermore through the coming years.

In the temple of Freedom, before its altar,
We kneel together side by side ;
Yet well we know that temple had fallen,
Except for those grand lives crucified.

Then sacred this day to Columbia's martyrs,
. Make lovely the graves of the noble slain ;
May freemen never their heritage barter,
Nor Freedom's altar with treason stain.

PROCLAMATION OF THE MAYOR.

On Saturday, the 29th of May, the memory of the gallant men who went out from our midst, and died in battle, or from disease, the result of hardship and exposure, is to be honored by decorating their graves with flowers, and other tokens of remembrance. It is right that by our presence and sympathy we should testify to their worth as citizens, to their heroic bravery as soldiers, and give evidence of our sorrow that we shall know them on earth no more. In this hour of peace and prosperity, all should honor those who reflected honor upon us and our city, in the day when the national life was in danger, by preserving and maintaining it intact and unbroken. They will not come back to us, but the noble work they have done remains to stimulate us to emulate their glorious deeds, and to ever honor their memory.

In accordance with the resolution adopted by the members of Post Greene, Grand Army Republic, of this city, and at the request of many citizens, I herewith issue my proclamation, most urgently requesting the citizens of Lansing, as befitting the occasion, to close their places of business from half-past one to four P. M., on Saturday afternoon, and to participate in the ceremonies of the day.

Given under my hand, at Lansing, on the 26th day of May, A. D. 1869.

CYRUS HEWITT, *Mayor.*

The ceremonies in this city, which were held under the direction of Post Greene, G. A. R., Comrade E. H. Porter, Senior Vice and Acting Commander, were peculiarly appropriate, and were largely attended, not only by residents of the city, but by people from neighboring towns; some who had been soldiers, and had stood bravely under the fire of shot and shell, coming more than twenty miles to join in the ceremonies. Long before noon the city was filled with strangers, and just before the hour of twelve a national salute gave notice to all that the exercises would not be postponed, as had been previously decided upon, owing to the storm of several days' duration.

In accordance with the proclamation of Mayor Hewitt, most of the business houses were closed, although several were too much interested in the acquisition of a stray dollar or two, to heed the request.

The procession formed at three o'clock P. M., headed by the Reform School Band, who were dressed in a new and tasty uniform. Fifteen ladies had been selected to distribute the flowers, many of whom were wives, sisters, or daughters of those who gave their lives for their country during the rebellion. These ladies headed the wagons in line, and were followed by not less than two hundred carriages and double teams. The band, on foot, were followed by the members of Post Greene, G. A. R., and other soldiers, and the firemen of the city, over one hundred strong, in uniform, and bearing the National banner, were also in line. Several hundred citizens on foot closed the procession, which made a fine and imposing appearance. On reaching the cemetery, several hundred people were already upon the ground, and the whole number present could not have been less than two thousand.

A beautiful cenotaph had been erected upon the hill on the western side of the cemetery, which was tastefully entwined with evergreens, flowers, and the National flag. Upon the base of this cenotaph, were the names of many soldiers who enlisted in this city, and fell in the field, or died in hospital, or the prison pens of the South, and whose bodies lie unnoticed and

unknown, far from home and friends. The following comprise
the names of this list, which is by no means complete, as there
was neither time nor means of gaining full and accurate
information:

Elisha Harrington,	A. C. Winter,
Thomas Perry,	Capt. Geo. Ellis,
Frederick Terrell,	Charles Foster,
William Alexander,	E. F. Siverd,
Lt. Jerome Beardsley,	Major Smith,
Capt. Jeffers,	Henry Meyer,
Capt. Mason,	Cyrus W. Coryell,
Daniel Shattuck,	Mathew Patrick,
Samuel Dowell,	Capt. J. B. Lafferty,
Silas Beebe,	John Schleicher,
Lieut. William Greene,	W. T. Hogan,
Peter Van Etter,	J. E. Elliott,
Edwin Lathrop,	Silas Thurston,
Thomas Cronk,	Farrell Conley,
Milo Smith,	Thomas Davenport,
John A. Douglas,	Charles Church,
Augustus Stearns,	James A. Ballard,
C. Haverland,	Calvin B. Holmes,
Frazer F. Smalley,	William Agard,
R. D. Wheeler,	Burt Hudson,
J. Sister,	I. Sweeny,
Mark Child,	H. C. Guest.

Upon the four sides of the base of the monument were the
following inscriptions:

" We died that our Country might Live."
" Remember our Children."
" Honor to our Absent Ones."
" Died in Battle."

Immediately upon the arrival of the procession at the Cemetery, after an appropriate prayer by the Rev. W. H. Perrine,
the decoration of the graves took place, under the direction of
E. H. Porter, Commandant of the Post. Over sixty veteran
soldiers, many of them scarred and disabled, joined in this
token of grateful remembrance. Upon each tomb-stone was
hung an evergreen wreath by the young ladies, who first scattered flowers upon the tomb, and then each soldier added his
flower tribute. At each grave thus decorated (thirteen in all)
was a tablet, giving name of the deceased and battles in which
he was engaged, and other known particulars. The cenotaph

and tablets, which were very beautiful and tasty, were designed by Major Abram Cottrell, of this city.

The following gives the inscriptions and the names of the dead soldiers whose graves were honored:

Mathew Elder, commissioned Capt. 8th Regiment Michigan Infantry, U. S. V., Aug. 12th, 1861. Commissioned by President, 1st Lieut. 11th Infantry U. S. A., Aug. 5th, 1862. Participated in the following engagements: Bombardment of Port Royal, battle of the Coosaw, and honorably mentioned by the Commanding General, I. I. Stevens; bombardment of Fort Pulaski, Chancellorville, and Gettysburg, where he was mortally wounded and died near the battle-field.

George D. Lathrop, enlisted Co. "B," 3d Regiment Michigan Infantry U. S. V.'s. Died Aug. 5th, 1864.

William A. Calkins, enlisted Co. "A," 20th Regiment Michigan Infantry U. S. V., Aug. 14th, 1862.

Edgar Yawger, enlisted Co. "G," 12th Regiment Michigan Infantry U. S. V.'s. Participated in the battle of Shiloh. Died at home from disease caused by the explosion of a shell.

Cephas B. Johnson, enlisted in 8th Regiment Michigan Infantry U. S. V.'s. Died May 31st, 1867.

J. J. Whitman, commissioned 1st Lieutenant 2d Regiment Berdan Sharpshooters, and promoted Capt. at 2d battle Bull Run, Aug., 1863, and was mortally wounded at the battle of South Mountain, Sept., 1863.

Elisha B. Mosher, enlisted in Co. "A," 20th Mich. Infantry U. S. Vol.'s Aug. 9th, 1862. Participated in the following engagements: Fredericksburg, Horse-Shoe Bend, Siege of Knoxville, Coal Harbor, Blue Springs, Turkey Bend, Wilderness, Spottsylvania, and North Anna. Was taken prisoner Sept. 30th, 1864; remained in prison at Andersonville 4 months; was paroled, came home, and soon died from effects of his imprisonment, April 17th, 1865.

Asahel W. Nichols, commissioned Capt. 1st Regiment Michigan Sharpshooters May 8th, 1863; promoted Major October 18th, 1864; promoted Lieut. Col. March 9th, 1865; brevetted Col. for conspicuous gallantry in the assault before Petersburgh, where he was severely wounded—died January 18th, 1866.

A. H. P. Morehouse, enlisted in Co. "A," 20th Regiment Michigan Infantry U. S. V., Aug. 9th, 1862. Died in hospital at Alexandria, Va., Dec. 13th, 1862.

Henry V. Hinckley, enlisted in Co. "A," 20th Regiment Michigan

Infantry, Aug. 9th, 1862. Promoted 2d Lieut. 1st Regiment Michigan Sharpshooters Feb. 19th, 1863. Promoted Captain Sept. 14th, 1864. Died in the spring of 1868.

Edwin J. Lathrop, enlisted Co. "II," 5th Michigan Cavalry. Died March 21st, 1865.

Artemas Baldwin, enlisted Co. "E," 8th Regiment Michigan Infantry U. S. V. Promoted through all the grades in the regular line of promotion up to Captain. Participated in the following engagements: Port Royal, Coosaw, Fort Pulaski, James Island, 2d Bull Run, Antietam, Wilderness, Spottsylvania, and surrender of Petersburg. Came home with his Regiment at the close of the war. Died Dec., 1867.

Charles S. Hunt, enlisted 2d Regiment Berdan's Sharpshooters; was taken prisoner at the battle of the Wilderness; imprisoned at Andersonville; paroled, and died at Annapolis, Md., on his way home, from the effects of his imprisonment.

EXERCISES AT THE STAND.

At the conclusion of the decoration of the graves, the assembly congregated on the hillside sloping to the eastward from the base of the cenotaph, and forming a natural amphitheatre, at the foot of which in the centre was the speaker's stand. The exercises here were opened by an impressive and appropriate prayer by Rev. Geo. H. Hickox, after which the choir of young men under the lead and direction of Prof. Hintz, sang a beautiful ode.

ORATION, BY COMRADE I. M. CRAVATH.

Comrades and Friends:

We are assembled to-day to honor by appropriate ceremonies, the memory of the nation's dead.

The Romans were wont to place statues of their dead heroes in the porches and passage-ways of their dwellings, so that, day by day, when they went out and when they came in, when they sat down and when they rose up, marble forms might speak to them, in mute but impressive language, of the names and deeds of those whom they would have in perpetual remembrance.

By such memorial services as we witness on this occasion, the soldiers of the Republic would perpetuate the remembrance of their fallen comrades; bound to them as they are by the recollections of common dangers and achievements, by friendships "born in peril, nourished by hardships, baptized in blood," and by the brotherhood of the cause and country which they laid down their lives to uphold.

The pillars of a nation's power rest on the graves of its defenders. As "the blood of the martyr's is the seed of the church," so the bodies of brave men, sown thick in the furrows of war, are the seed from which springs national existence. In a land like ours, where the "common consent" must "provide for the common defense," the patriotism of the people is the rock of the nation's strength. Without this, her domain, however broad, would be defenseless, and her resources, however great, would be only the tempting prey of the spoiler.

The test of patriotism is the readiness with which a people respond to the call of their country in her hour of danger, their endurance of trials and sacrifices in her behalf, and the bravery with which they meet and beat back her foes, on land and sea, in the trenches and "the imminent deadly breach."

The patriotism exhibited by the American people, during the gigantic struggle which closed four years ago, has filled the world with wonder. Monarchists, profoundly convinced that the result of the great rebellion would be the dismemberment of the great Republic, watched with grim satisfaction the humiliation which they supposed awaited the last great experiment of the people in the science of government—that study deemed only a fit occupation for kings.

While praise is due in no stinted measure to all classes of the loyal people of this country, to those who poured their wealth into the nation's treasury, to those who gave their husbands, brothers and sons to their country's service, and proved in ten thousand ways, their patriotic devotion, yet her citizen soldiers are the crowning glory of the Republic.

While the cloud of war grew dark in the southern sky, sending forth the muttering thunder of the coming storm, while traitors in high places plotted treason, betraying our counsels, bankrupting our credit, surrendering to the enemy our handful of an army, and scattering our fleet to the four quarters of the earth, our citizen soldiers, busy with the avocations of peaceful life, calmly waited the hour when their country called them to the rescue. When that call came, how the mighty multitude rose up and swept on like ocean waves, white with the fury of the storm! how their patriotism kindled at the disgraceful rout at Bull's Run, survived the murder at Ball's Bluff, the disastrous defeats of the Peninsular campaign, and the bloody carnage of Chickamauga; how they stemmed the tide of rebel victories, and rolled back defeat on the foe at Antietam, at Shiloh, at Stone River, at Winchester and at Gettysburgh; how they carried our "star spangled banner" from the Wilderness to Richmond, from Atlanta to the sea, from Donelson to Vicksburg; how they bore it up the heights of Mission Ridge, made luminous for all time by the lustre of their deeds of valor, and higher still, till from the lofty crest of Lookout Mountain it floated out above the clouds into the serene sunshine of heaven; all these, and more, are matters of history. To-day the flag of our country floats over a land undivided, a Union saved, a government vindicated, a people free. As it waves above us in the calm atmosphere of peace, it seems transfigured by the mighty deeds that shed upon it unfading glory, and clothe it with an influence that shall one day loose the bands of despotism in other lands than ours, and open the gates of power throughout the world to the triumphant march of human freedom.

Death is but an accident in the career of the brave. They die that the Nation may live; but while the Nation lives, they shall live also—live with their names inscribed on her roll of honor, live with their deeds recorded on the pages of her history, live in the heroism inspired by their example, live in the blessings purchased by their death.

But every soldier, who acted well his part, who faced the enemy with unflinching firmness, who presented his body as a shield to protect his home, his kindred and his country, is justly entitled to the gratitude of his countrymen, whether he be standing among the living, or sleeping with the dead. They braved a common danger, they faced a common foe; but the one was taken, and the other left. They who sleep beneath these grassy mounds have been gathered by the reaper of the harvest into the Nation's garner, while yonder stand the sheaves that remain.

Comrades! You who have proved your bravery on many battle-fields; you who have shed your blood to save your country, and mingled your flesh with the dust of the fallen; you who stand with one foot among the living and the other among the dead; you who have laid down your *arms* never to take them up again; yours be the post of honor among men, so long as gratitude shall dwell in the hearts of your countrymen, and you wear the badge of honorable scars!

But the scenes that surround us, and the ceremonies that we have witnessed, remind me that we are gathered here, not to eulogize the living, but to pay such tribute as we may to the memory of the fallen.

We stand within the confines of the city of the dead—that buried city, whose grass-grown roofs and marble spires rise to view to mark the resting places of the departed, whose streets are trod by forms unseen by mortals, and whose gates are closed day and night, because the dwellers therein, like Rome when the temple of Janus was shut, are forever at peace with the world.

Yonder sleeps the dust of WHITMAN—first of the returning brave whose brows were crowned with the chaplet of immortality. Yonder lies all that is mortal of ELDER, laid low by a shaft of death on the field of Gettysburg. There rests the wasted form of HUNT, who met a cruel fate at the hands of an inhuman foe. Here, too, are the ashes of MOREHOUSE and PADDLEFORD, of NICHOLS and HINCKLEY, friends in life and companions in death; of MOSHER, BALDWIN, LATHROP, HUDSON, JOHNSON, CALKINS, SISTEN, YAWGER, and others, brave men all, whose graves fair hands, this day, have strewed with flowers bedewed with tears. Nor do we forget the lamented

AGARD,	EVERETT,	PERRY,
ALEXANDER,	FOSTER,	SCHLEICHER,
BALLARD,	GREENE,	SHATTUCK,
BEARDSLEY,	GUEST,	SISTER,
BEEBE,	HARRINGTON,	SIVERD,
CHILD,	HAVERLAND,	SMALLEY,
CHURCH,	HOGAN,	SMITH, M.,
CONLEY,	HOLMES,	SMITH, J. H.,
CORYELL,	HUDSON,	STEARNS,
CRONK,	JEFFERS,	SWEENY,
DAVENPORT,	LAFFERTY,	TERRELL,
DAVIS,	LATHROP,	THURSTON,
DOUGLAS,	MASON,	TURNER,
DOWELL,	MEYER,	VAN ETTER,
ELLIS,	OATLEY,	WHEELER,
ELLIOTT,	PATRICK,	WINTER,

And all that long list of honored names, for whom, as we call the muster roll of the nation's dead heroes, we cannot answer that they are "here." On distant battle-fields they lie,—in trenches piled with corpses,—in the "deep sea,"—in unknown graves. Wherever their dust reposes, their names are cherished in the grateful recollections of their countrymen, and their memory is written in the hearts of those who mourn for them like Rachel weeping for her children, and will not be comforted because they are not.

Peace be your portion, O, departed spirits of the nation's dead! God grant that in the hour of your mortal agony, when the fainting spirit let go its hold on the crumbling clay, you were permitted to drink of that fountain of living water, of which if a man drink he shall never thirst; and thus, clothed with the vigor of eternal youth, you pitched your white tents in the Grand Encampment of the blessed, forever beyond the reach of " the noise of battle and the alarm of war."

How quiet are the dwellings of our fallen comrades! How calm is their long repose!

"They sleep their last sleep,
They have fought their last battle,
No sound can awake them to glory again."

And yet, as we repeat their names; as the recollections with which they are associated throng upon us, how their well-remembered features come back to us again, and their familiar voices sound once more in our ears! As we summon them at the roll-call of memory, the passionless dust of the sleepers stirs with awakening life; their graves open, and they come forth, clad not in the habiliments of the tomb, but in garments of living flesh. From distant battle-fields they come with hurrying feet, and take their accustomed places among us. The sea gives up its dead, and the dark shadow that rests on an unknown fate yields up the forms of the "missing." Once more they stand before their country's altar and swear allegiance to her cause. Once more they mingle in the scenes of the camp, of dress-parade, of battalion drill, and march side by side with us to the field of bloody strife. Again the battle is set. Here stand the Union lines; yonder the ranks of rebel soldiery. Steadily the contending hosts feel their way toward each other beneath a canopy of smoke that thickens above them into a cloud lurid with lightning and dense with the leaden, iron hail of the storm. Now the rebels charge with fiendish yell on the ranks of the boys in blue, who meet the shock unmoved, and beat them back as the rock beats back the waves of the turbulent sea. Now the Union lines advance, and the foe are driven before that serried front of bristling bayonets as the chaff of the threshing-floor is driven before the whirlwind. While through all these shifting scenes, and filling the pauses between, the zip of rifle and musket-balls, the bursting of bombs, the shriek of careering shells, and the thunder of earth-shaking cannon, make strange music to unaccustomed ears, and, mingling their voices together in one sublime chorus, send forth on the wings of the wind the awful, mighty roar of battle.

The scene changes. Cold on the "field of the dead" lie the thickly strewed bodies of the slain, their half-shut, sightless eyes full of unconscious wonder at the spirit's untimely flight; or, among the wounded, piled like stranded drifts on the shore of the red sea of war; or, in comfortless hospitals, where they were consumed by the hot breath of fever, or poisoned by pestilence engendered by half-buried corpses; or, in horrid prison-pens, where they died of slow starvation and agonies unutterable, with no friendly hand to smooth their hard earth-pillow, and lead their shelterless souls down their rugged path into the dark valley. As we recount these scenes of hardship, suffering, and death through which they passed, the very air above us seems damp with death-dew and murky with measureless, brooding horrors. Though, while life remained, their hearts pined most of all, and with indescribable longing for a sight of the loved ones they were never to look upon with mortal vision, and of homes whither their feet were never more to return, yet, through every changing event their fortitude changed not, and lights up even the gloom of their untimely fate with star-like, imperishable glory. For this, let their graves be strewed with flowers on each returning year, so long as the tree of liberty which they watered with their blood, and which stretches out its sheltering arms in blessings on our country, shall grow in majesty, in greatness, and in the perfection of beauty.

How vast the multitude of the nation's dead! exceeded in number in the history of the world only by the host Darius mustered on the plain of Arbela, or Xerxes marched across the Hellespont; and for which Michigan furnished an army-corps of twenty thousand men! Were this vast throng of the departed, this Grand Army of the Republic, to pass by day's marches along our streets, we could, for nearly six successive days, were our eyes but opened to behold the sight, see that long line of shadowy forms march on with steady steps and streaming banners to the bivouac of the dead.

But these were only part of the price paid for the purchase and preservation of our liberties. What sorrow sits clothed in sackcloth in homes whose light has gone out forever! where sons and brothers have been given up one by one to feed the bloody sacrifice of war; where husbands and fathers went forth with the "unreturning brave," leaving wives desolate and children fatherless!

Here we pause. Before grief like this it becomes us to stand with silent lips and uncovered heads. We leave the stricken ones to the tender mercy of Him who "sticketh closer than a brother, who is the Father of the fatherless and the widow's God," and the stay and the staff of those whose earthly hopes lie buried in the graves of their children.

Thus we have a glimpse of the price that was paid for the purchase of our free institutions—a price that cannot be counted in gold, nor weighed in diamonds. How precious, then, should they be to us, the heirs of so priceless a heritage! With what vigilance should we guard them from peril and corruption! How clean should be the hands that are permitted to handle the ark of the covenant of our liberties! How great and pure should be the men to whose keeping we intrust "the peace and the good name and the happiness of a people whose salvation was cheap, even at the price that was paid!" If there be money-changers found in our national temple—men who buy and sell the places of public trust like stocks on 'change, and the people like cattle in the market place, let them be driven out under the lash of public scorn, and their places filled by men worthy to minister at such an altar!

Americans! Be true to yourselves, to your country, and to God, and prove yourselves worthy of the exalted privileges vouchsafed to you as a people! By the signal blessings bestowed on this fair land of ours; by the terrible judgments poured out in wrath upon us for our national sins; from the sepulchres of buried nations; from the wrecks that float on the dead sea of the past to mark the spot where great ships went down, freighted with treasures of peoples that were, but are not; in history, in His providence, and in His Sacred Word, God speaks to you with a Trinity of voices, saying: "Righteousness exalteth a nation;" "But if they will not obey, I will utterly pluck up and destroy that nation, saith the Lord."

Let us remember that to live a noble, spotless life, is better than to die a glorious death; that national sins are but the aggregate of individual sins; and that there is One who marks with sleepless eyes the deeds of men, and who will "bring every work into judgment, with every secret thing, whether it be good or whether it be evil." ·

> "So live, that when thy summons comes to join
> The innumerable caravan, which moves
> To that mysterious realm, where each shall take
> His chamber in the silent halls of death,
> Thou go not, like the quarry-slave at night,
> Scourged to his dungeon, but sustained and soothed
> By an unfaltering trust"

in Jesus Christ—the Savior of men, and healed of every infirmity, cleansed of every stain, and purified of every sin,— white-robed immortals shall strew flowers of fadeless beauty along your march to that city, where your glorified feet shall keep time to the song of the redeemed; that city, where "there shall be no more death, neither sorrow nor crying, neither shall there be any more pain;" that city, which hath "no need of the sun, neither of the moon, to shine in it," for the Lord God Almighty is "the temple of it," "and the Lamb is the light thereof."

The oration was followed by music from the band, another ode from the choir, and a closing prayer by Rev. J. Straub, after which the procession re-formed and returned to the city. The veteran "Boys in Blue" here gave three cheers for the band, three for the ladies, and three for the firemen of Lansing, and the large crowd dispersed.

Those who had the affair in direction are to be congratulated upon its perfection, and the precision and good taste with which the exercises were conducted.

On Sunday, May 30th, able and effective sermons were preached by Rev. Geo. H. Hickox, pastor of the First Baptist Church; by Rev. Stewart Sheldon, pastor of the Plymouth Congregational Church, and by Rev. J. Straub, pastor of the First Universalist Church.

In the neighboring village of Okemos, suitable ceremonies were observed on the morning of the 29th, Elder A. Rolfe and Capt. T. F. Powers participating in the exercises.

LAPEER.

The observances were held in this village the 29th of May, under the direction of Post Turrill, G. A. R., Maynard Butts, commanding. The procession formed at one o'clock P. M., at Post Headquarters, headed by the Cornet Band, marched to the Union School House, and escorted a delegation of young ladies to the M. E. Church, where an excellent address was delivered by Rev. A. R. Bartlett. At the close of the services at the church, the procession re-formed, and, headed by the clergymen, and accompanied by the citizens, and the booming of a cannon firing minute guns, marched to the Cemetery, where the ceremony of strewing the graves with flowers was duly performed by groups of young ladies,—one group for each grave—the comrades halting, opening their ranks at each grave for the group to pass through, perform the ceremony, and return to the rear.

The procession was over one-fourth of a mile in length, and everything passed off in the most satisfactory manner to all.

MARSHALL.

The Decoration occurred in this city on Saturday, May 29th, with great success. The day was pleasant, and at a very early hour people from the country began to fill State street, and their number constantly increased until the moving of the procession, which was organized at 10:30 A. M., and passed up State street to the Cemetery, in the following order:

1. Marshall Cornet Band.
2. Escort—Marshall Commandery.
3. Officers and Speaker.
4. The Ladies' Committee on Decoration.
5. The Common Council.
6. The Fire Department.
7. Blue Lodge and Royal Arch Masons of the city.

8. Masonic Delegations from Bellevue and Tekonsha.
9. Peninsular Lodge I. O. of O. F.
10. German Benevolent Society.
11. Citizens on foot and in carriages.

The display was the. finest ever seen in the city. The civic societies generously responded to the invitation,—over three hundred Masons being in the procession.

The programme at the Cemetery was as follows:

1. Music—Dirge.
2. Prayer, by the Chaplain.
3. Music.
4. Oration, by Capt. J. C. Burrows.
5. Music.
6. Benediction, by Rev. Mr. St. John.

During the Dirge, the graves of the Soldiers who sleep in the city Cemetery were decorated. The number of mounds thus the objects of patriotic regard, are twenty-six, as follows:

INFANTRY REGIMENTS.

Capt. W. S. Woodruff, 1st.
Hiram Daily, 3d.
Oliver Van Zandt, 4th.
Henry Bostock, 6th.
Seymour W. Davis, 6th.
George Raymond, 6th.
Alexander T. Craig, 6th.
George Bostock, 10th.
Robert H. Paxton,* 13th.
Capt. H. F. Robinson, 20th.
James McRoberts,* 20th.
Cady Rowley, Engineers & Mechanics.
Daniel VanValin, "   "
Capt. G. A. Woodruff, 4th U. S. Artillery.
Robert McRoberts,* 4th N. Y. Battery.
Capt. John VanArman, Illinois Regiment.
John Pendleton, Illinois Regiment.
W. H. Hinkle, Illinois Regiment.

* Buried South, but have tombs in the Cemetery.

Daniel Murdock, 2d.
A. H. Craig, 8th.
J. L. Schmidt, 8th.
Lieut. Edwin Savacool, 1st N. Y.
Sidney Taft, unknown.
—— Connor, unknown.

In order to recall the services of those of our soldiery who died in the South and rest far from their Northern homes, a CENOTAPH was erected, decked with evergreens and flags, on which were displayed the following inscriptions:

"To the memory of our Patriot Dead, who sleep in distant fields."
"Our land is glory's still, and theirs."
"The path of duty is the way to glory."
"Bright be the place of their souls."

"On fame's eternal camping ground
Their silent tents are spread,
And Glory guards with solemn round,
The bivouac of the dead!"

"The hopes, the fears, the blood, the tears
That marked the bitter strife,
Are now all crowned with victory
That saved the Nation's life."

"Nor wreck, nor change, nor winter's blight,
Nor time's remorseless doom,
Shall mar one ray of Glory's light
That gilds their sacred tomb."

"The fittest place where Man can die,
Is where he dies for Man."

The tasteful oration of Capt. J. C. Burrows was the subject of much commendation. Very properly brief, it guided the minds of the hearers very naturally to the gallant services of the patriotic dead, and by which they, though dead, still speak to us. We do well to guard their memory and lavish such floral gifts upon their graves,—let us guard their tombs with a jealous care, and prove ourselves proper heritors of their bravery and patriotism. A shaft should be reared whose sides should enumerate their deeds and preach of their sacrifices for Liberty.

Upon the conclusion of the address the procession re-organized and proceeded to the Catholic Cemetery, where are the graves of Dennis Cronin, of the 28th Infantry, and James Brady, of the Navy. Having laid flowers upon the graves of these brave Irishmen, the procession returned to the Court House and was dismissed.

———◆———

MONROE.

The services occurred in this city on Sunday, May 30th. Nearly two thousand persons were present at the ceremonies in Woodland Cemetery. The eulogy was delivered by Hon. Edwin Willits, and a poem suitable to the occasion was recited by Hon. E. G. Morton. Taking into consideration the decidedly unpleasant state of the weather, the celebration may be set down as an entire success.

———◆———

NILES.

List of soldiers' graves decorated in Silver Creek Cemetery:

James Pullman, Private, 6th Michigan Infantry.
C. S. Taggard, " 11th " Cavalry.
Charles Richardson, Musician, 6th Michigan Infantry.
Eli A. Griffin, Major, 19th Michigan Infantry.
Don. Clark, Private, 25th Michigan Infantry.
J. R. Cunningham, Private, 17th Michigan Infantry.
Frank Earle, Private, 27th Michigan Infantry.
A. L. Stites, Sergeant, 25th Michigan Infantry.
Charles Woodruff, Adjutant, 25th Michigan Infantry.
Cyrus Bacon, Surgeon, U. S. A.
William Phillipps, Sergeant, 8th Michigan Cavalry.
G. Stites, 25th Michigan Infantry.
H. P. Glenn, Sergeant, 6th Michigan Infantry.
George A. Hunt, Private, 6th Michigan Infantry.
William Casby, 23d Massachusetts Volunteers.
Wm. Henderson, Regiment unknown.
A. C. Ford, " "
M. Piggin, " "

OLIVET.

The ceremonies here took place on May 30th, under the direction of the citizen-soldiers of the place, there being no Post of the G. A. R. established here. Although very rainy, a large audience was in attendance at the church. Soldiers, and friends of deceased soldiers occupied the central pews.

Two beautiful shields, draped in black, hung back of the desk, surrounded by the National colors. On one of these was inscribed, "Our Fallen Heroes;" on the other, "Frank Hosford, our Ministering Angel!" in memory of the loved and patriotic daughter of "Father Hosford," and sister of our worthy superintendent, who died while caring for our soldiers on Lookout Mountain. The exercises, presided over by S. A. Andrus, were introduced by an appropriate voluntary by the choir, who also sang, during the exercises, the two hymns written by William Oland Bourne. President Morrison read passages of scripture, and offered prayer. Rev. H. O. Ladd then delivered a very interesting address from the words, "So then, death worketh in us, but life in you." 2d Cor. 4: 12. The speaker proceeded to show in what ways the death of our heroes had given life to us as a nation, politically, socially, and morally. Instances of heroic death were narrated that brought back vividly the cost of our Nation's life. His tribute to the memory of Miss Hosford, and of the four soldiers who lie in our cemetery, was beautiful and touching.

After the address the audience, preceded by the band, repaired to the cemetery, over the entrance to which was an arch of evergreens encircling "In Memoriam." The soldiers and friends of the deceased then strewed the already decorated graves with flowers, an appropriate dirge by the band adding solemnity to the scene. All then joined in singing "Shall we gather at the River?" and, as the benediction was pronounced, felt that the day had not been desecrated in their quiet village by thus remembering our fallen heroes.

OVID.

The ceremonies at this place were observed May 30th, 1869, under the direction of Post No. 13, E. Nelson Fitch, Sen. Vice and Acting Commander, and in which the citizens of Ovid and vicinity united, under the command of W. C. Bennett, Esq. After a sermon appropriate to the occasion, delivered in Metropolitan Hall by Rev. H. A. Rose, at three o'clock P. M. the procession, headed by the brass band, marched to the village cemetery, and the graves of our deceased comrades were strewn with flowers by a committee of children selected for the purpose. A short address was delivered by Acting Commander E. N. Fitch, and the benediction was pronounced by Rev. John Martin, when the procession returned to the village. This is the second observance of the day by Post No. 13. Though the day was wet and dreary, the crowded hall, and the long line of citizens marching in the procession, attested their sympathy with the occasion.

PONTIAC.

Owing to the unfavorable weather, the ceremonies were postponed from May 29th to June 4th, when the weather proved still more unfavorable. Notwithstanding the rain, a goodly number of citizens in the order designated in the programme, and headed by the Pontiac Silver Cornet Band, marched up Saginaw street, to Clinton Hall, where the further observances of the day were carried out. The Hall was nearly filled with a patriotic assemblage, who, in the spirit of meekness, did homage to the brave patriots who died in defense of our country's flag.

The services were opened with prayer, by the Rev. W. H. McGiffert, followed by the choir singing a memorial hymn.

The oration, by Rev. W. H. Sheir, was able, and well received, and contained an eloquent eulogy on the departed

brave. He commenced by recalling to mind the great sacrifice
that was offered upon the altar of our common country; the
great struggle through which our nation has passed, costing
the lives of 350,000 Union soldiers, and 250,000 more, who
have been maimed and ruined. He said Michigan's contribution to the army was 90,747; 1,453 colored troops. Oak-
land county sent of this number, 3,718. Our final triumph,
the joy felt by the Union people throughout the country, their
manifestations, and then the dark pall which rested upon us
in the death of Abraham Lincoln, was most graphically
depicted. He then read the roll of the dead:

NAMES OF SOLDIERS AND SAILORS BURIED IN OAK HILL CEMETERY,
PONTIAC.

Major General I. B. Richardson, U. S. V., mortally wounded at
Antietam.

Colonel Moses Wisner, 22d Mich. Infantry, died at Lexington, Ky.

Captain T. C. Beardslee, 22d Mich. Infantry, died at Nashville, Tenn.

Private Turner Tompkinson, 22d Mich. Infantry, died at Lexington, Ky.

Color Sergeant T. Miller, 8th Mich. Infantry, died at home.

Lieutenant Samuel Pearce, 5th Mich. Infantry, killed at the crossing
of the North Anna, Va.

Sergeant Beckwith Capron, 5th Mich. Infantry, died at home.

Private Peter Dibeau, 5th Mich. Infantry, starved at Andersonville.
Buried in Catholic Cemetery.

Private John H. Carran, 5th Mich. Infantry, died at Camp Michigan,
Virginia.

Lieutenant Percy S. Leggett, 5th Mich. Cavalry, killed near the Rap-
pahannoc.

Lieutenant Richard Whitehead, 5th Mich. Cavalry, killed near Han-
over Court House.

Private George Wesson, 5th Mich. Infantry, died at home.

Drum Major —— Daniels, 5th Mich. Infantry, died at home.

Sergeant John Chamberlain, 10th Mich. Infantry, killed at Jones-
borough, Ga.

Private Lewis Eldred, died at home.

Private Lamont Pratt, 8th Mich. Cavalry, "missing," supposed to
have died at Andersonville.

Private Jonas Ladd, 2d Mich. Infantry, died at home.

16

Lieutenant Joseph McConnell, 18th U. S. Infantry, killed at Stone River.

Q. M. Sergeant Eugene Nelson, died at Nashville.

Sergeant Major William Churchill, 7th Mich. Infantry, killed at Antietam.

Captain William North, 5th Mich. Cavalry, killed at Cedar Creek, Va.

Private Arthur Pierce, 4th Mich. Infantry, died in Tennessee.

Private Jonathan Ash, died at home.

Private Hamilton Davis, 15th Mich. Infantry, killed at Atlanta, Ga.

Private Joseph Davis, 14th Mich. Infantry, mortally wounded at Chattahoochee River.

William Shaw, died at home.

James Stuart, 1st Colored Infantry, died at home.

Edward Stickney, 5th Mich. Cavalry, killed after his return home.

He stated there were 27 soldiers, ranking from a Major General down to a private, in our cemetery, and out of that number, he knew of but one who had nothing to mark his resting place, and that one was Maj. Gen. I. B. Richardson (or as he was more familiarly known in the army, "Fighting Dick.") He proceeded to state that the General was a graduate of West Point, and fought under Gen. Scott in all the important battles in the Mexican War, and as soon as the rebellion broke out was one of the first to offer his services to his country. He fought bravely in the Army of the Potomac up to the time he was killed, but after he had gained such a national reputation as a patriot and a fighting General, being one of the first made Major Generals. A stranger, desirous of visiting his grave, could not find it in our cemetery without the aid of a guide, as it remains up to this time wholly unmarked.

When he told of the reverence our brave boys had for the old flag, how they toiled and suffered by its inspirations, it brought tears to the eyes of many who best knew of the truth he was uttering.

The address throughout was most touching, and left a lasting impression upon the hearer.

The ceremonies were closed by singing by the choir, and the benediction by Rev. W. H. McGiffert. Arrangements had been so perfected, that, had the day been pleasant, the ceremony would have been exceedingly impressive. As it was, the procession, consisting of the Band, Knights Templar, Odd Fellows, Good Templars, in their various uniforms, the Steam Fire Engine and Hose Cart—the former drawn by horses, and the latter drawn by the members of the company, beautifully decorated with bouquets of flowers and draped with the American flag—together with the M. E. Church Sabbath school, with banners, on which were inscribed the mottoes—"Honor to our Brave Defenders," "God is our Refuge and Strength," presented a very creditable appearance.

SCHOOLCRAFT.

The exercises at Schoolcraft occurred on Sunday, May 30th. A procession was formed at half-past 2 p. m., in the following order, under the direction of the Marshal:

1st. Officer of the Day, J. T. Cobb, Esq.
2d. Schoolcraft Silver Cornet Band.
3d. Speaker and Chaplain.
4th. Eight Misses, dressed in white, each bearing a wreath and vase of flowers, with which to decorate the graves (eight in number) of our deceased soldiers.
5th. Soldiers.
6th. Citizens.

The procession then marched, slowly and in good order, from the church to the cemetery, under the sweet, inspiring and elevating music of the band. Entering through the gate, under a flag gracefully festooned and ornamented with flowers, proceeded to a stand erected in one corner of the grounds, from which the exercises took place, in the following order:

1st. A fervent and appropriate prayer by the Chaplain, Rev. N. Rice.
2d. Singing by the Glee Club.
3d. Music by the Band.
4th. Address and reading of the Ode prepared for the occasion, by Hon. E. L. Brown.

5th. Singing the Ode, to music arranged by Jonas Allen, Esq., with introduction and interlude by the Band.

6th. Marching of the procession to each grave, preceded by the Band, while playing a solemn and impressive dirge, composed for the occasion by Prof. Dresskell, and followed by the girls, with wreaths and flowers.

Each one, as she approached a soldier's grave, placed a wreath at the head and a bouquet of flowers at the feet of the sleeping hero, and then falling in the rear of her sisters as they passed, and in this way making the whole circuit until all were decorated by their delicate hands. An arch of evergreens, erected at the head of each grave, with a cross of the same suspended in the center and decorated also with flowers, had been previously arranged by the good taste of the ladies of the committee. The benediction was then pronounced by Rev. N. Rice. All present appeared to realize the importance of the hour, and no other occasion could have induced so large an audience, and especially ladies, to remain during the exercises in an unceasing rain.

The following is an extract from the address of Hon. E. L. Brown:

Not like the nations of old do we celebrate the victory, with captors chained to the chariot wheels of the victor, in long and mournful procession, to meet the taunts and insults of an excited and exulting populace; but they who had scorned, defied, and assaulted the government of their country, restored to its kindly and protecting care, and to the homes and the rights they had forfeited; in the quiet pursuits of the arts of peace, in a community of rights, civil and political, for all under its banner learn to respect its power, to honor its justice, and to love its beneficence, while we, the victors, as mourners rather, come with hearts at once sad and exultant, to crown with flowers and undying laurel the brows of those

" Whose wounds for us this long-wish'd rest obtained,
And peace and freedom for their country gained."

There now sleep in this cemetery, over whose graves we come

to perform this sadly-pleasing ceremony, eight of those who went out from among us to do battle for their country's right and honor, slain in battle by the accidents and exposures of war, or miserably perished in consequence of the most barbarous treatment in captivity. Their names, regiments, date and manner of their death, are as follows:

Daniel F. Miller, Sergeant Company L, 5th Mich. Cavalry, wounded in action, near Richmond, Va., May 11th, 1864. Died of a wound at Point Lookout, Md., June 15th, 1864; aged 24 years.

Joseph Burson, Company L, 5th Michigan Cavalry, killed in action at Hawes' Shop, Va., May 28th, 1864; aged 22 years.

Abner II. Burson, Company L, 5th Michigan Cavalry, captured at Trevillian Station, Va., June 11th, 1864; imprisoned at Andersonville; liberated November 26th; came home, and died from the effects of starvation, February 24th, 1865; aged 27 years.

Lieut. Frank Corbyn, Company I, 3d Michigan Cavalry, wounded in a charge at Water Valley, Miss., December 18th, 1862; died of wounds at Lagrange, Tenn., January 11th, 1863; aged 26 years.

Charles Adair, killed by the accidental discharge of a musket July 4, 1863; aged 20 years.

Geo. Thompson, Corporal Company D, 17th Michigan Infantry, died from disease contracted in the service, February 18, 1866; aged 24 years.

Albert Chapman, Sergeant Company C, 6th Michigan Infantry; contracted disease in the service; arrived home October 21st, 1863, and died October 25th, 1864.

Albion Smith, of the 11th Michigan Infantry, returned and died in this village. I have no further knowledge of the facts concerning him.

Besides these of our fellow citizens who fell in the great rebellion, and are buried here, the following are the names of some of those who, from this immediate neighborhood, followed their country's flag, and fell gloriously, their bodies remaining in the far South, on the field of their glory:

First Lieut. Charles Pursel, killed in action at Averysboro, North Carolina, March 16th, 1865, in the very hour of victory, and almost the last shot of the rebellion; Mathew Smith, Henry Beals, John Kline, John Briggs, and William Firney.

At so great a cost to every village and hamlet throughout all the Northern States was the honor, and authority, and unity of the Nation sustained and defended. Let the youth who mark the honors justly conferred upon the victims, learn to emulate their examples.

STURGIS.

The soldiers of Sturgis performed the customary rites on Sunday, May 30th, under the direction of Gen. Wm. L. Stoughton. After the ceremonies at the Cemetery, a large assembly met at Union Hall, where the following exercises were held:

1. Singing a patriotic song by the ladies.
2. Prayer by Rev. Mr. Temple.
3. Singing by the young ladies.
4. Oration by Mr. J. R. Davies.
5. Benediction by Rev. Mr. Brown.

TECUMSEH.

Sermons were preached on Memorial Day in the Universalist, Presbyterian, and Methodist churches, respectively, by Rev. J. M. H. Smith, Rev. W. J. Stoutenberg, and Rev. L. H. Dean. After morning services were over in the different churches, as the clouds seemed to be breaking away, the procession formed in line and proceeded to the Cemetery.

Here the programme as published was carried out, although it began to rain soon after arriving at the ground. After the ceremonies at the stand, which were music by the Band, and an address by Mr. Boyd, the assembly, headed by the little girls with wreaths, and surviving soldiers bearing bouquets, repaired to the soldiers' graves to decorate them. We subjoin the record of those whose graves were decorated:

Warren Estes, enlisted in Co. E, 18th Mich. Vol. Infantry. Died at Tecumseh, April 4, 1868, of disease contracted in the service.

John Culbertson, Company I, 5th Mich. Vol. Infantry. Died at Tecumseh, Dec. 2d, 1867, of disease contracted in the service.

Faron Anderson, enlisted in Company B, 2d Mich. Vol. Infantry. Killed in rifle pits before Petersburg, Va., July 15th, 1864.

John G. Gilbert, Company G, 25th Mich. Vol. Infantry. Died at Louisville,'Ky.

Alanson Conkling, 2d Lieut. 7th Mich. Battery. Died at Vicksburg, Miss., Feb. 15th, 1863.

Wm. A. McCaughen, Company I, 18th Mich. Vols. Died at Nashville, Tenn., Feb. 4, 1864.

James R. Wheeler, Company E, 18th Mich. Vols. Died at Tecumseh,
of disease contracted in the service.

Charles F. Doke, 1st Sergeant Co. B, 8th Mich. Cavalry. Died at
Tecumseh, May 21, 1866.

Morris Roberts, Lieut. Co. F, 26th Mich. Vols. Died in Hospital at
Alexandria, Va., Sept. 14th, 1864.

Henry W. Stout, Co. E, 18th Mich. Vols. Died at Tecumseh, of
disease contracted in the service.

Henry J. Ladd, Captain of Cavalry.

Emory Waller, Co. F, 26th Mich. Vols. Died in Hospital at Alexandria, Va., Sept. 3, 1863.

Martin V. B. Pennock, Corporal Co. G, 4th Mich. Infantry. Died
Jan. 6, 1864.

Samuel D. Southworth.

THREE RIVERS.

At 2 o'clock P. M., May 30th, the comrades of Prutzman
Post, No. 44, G. A. R., assembled at their headquarters in
Prutzman's Hall. After listening to the reading of orders,
they were formed and marched to Kelsey's Hall, preceded by
the Three Rivers Cornet Band. The comrades wore white
gloves, and had crape on the left arm; the three senior officers
wore red crape across the right shoulder, with a knot of white
and blue ribbon at the breast; the Post Surgeon and Assistant
Surgeon General wore green sashes; the other officers wore
blue scarfs, with knot of white and red ribbon; the other
comrades, white scarfs with knot of red and blue ribbon. In
the ranks were carried the battle-worn and tattered standards
of the 11th Michigan Volunteers, donated by Gen. Stoughton
for the occasion. The Post presented a fine appearance, their
soldierly bearing and measured tread recalling the days, and
awakening the spirit of 1861. Kelsey's Hall, tastefully decorated with wreaths, crosses and bouquets, was crowded to its

utmost capacity by our citizens. At 3 P. M. the sound of the gavel called the assemblage to order, and all throughout the services the most profound silence prevailed, all seeming deeply impressed with the solemnity of the occasion.

The exercises were opened by an ode, written for the occasion, sung by Mrs. Grace Snyder and Mr. Henry G. Gregory; this was followed by a prayer by Rev. W. H. Pierce; next came a dirge by the band; then the address by comrade W. H. H. Wilcox. After the address, the audience joined in singing the hymn "My Country 'tis of thee—;" prayer was then offered by Rev. J. A. Ranney, and benediction invoked by Rev. Mr. Goodall. At the close of these services, the procession was re-formed and marched to Riverside Cemetery in the following order:

Post Commander and Officer of the Day.
Cornet Band.
Escort of Honor, consisting of twelve Comrades with Reversed Arms, commanded by the Post Adjutant.
Post Chaplain and Clergy.
Comrades of Post No. 44, bearing flowers.
Soldiers and Sailors of the late War.
Citizens and others, on foot and in Carriages.

As the command "March" was given, the rain ceased falling, and during the ceremonies at the cemetery the sun was shining, as if in token of the Divine approval of the tribute paid to the noble dead.

Arriving at the cemetery, the procession found hundreds of citizens waiting there to unite in the decorations of the soldiers' graves. The graves, ten in number, were marked by small flags, the national colors, surmounted by a streamer of crape. The comrades of the G. A. R. were marched around the cemetery, halting at each of the graves above mentioned, and strewing them with flowers. After all the graves had been thus decorated, the Post was formed upon the soldier's monumental lot, in a hollow square, in the center of which was erected a mound of flowers in honor of those dead comrades whose remains repose on southern soil. The ceremonies were concluded by the escort firing three volleys of musketry as a salute of honor. The Post then returned to their headquarters and were dismissed. From sunrise until sunset the national colors were flying at half-mast from the Post Headquarters and from the Reporter Office. In the morning, sermons appropriate to the day were delivered by the clergy of the village.

WAYNE.

Memorial Day was duly observed in this village, on Sunday, May 30th. At 11 o'clock A. M., a very able and patriotic address was made in the Methodist Church by Rev. J. W. McIlwain, the chaplain of the day, and soon thereafter, although the rain came down in torrents nearly all day, a long procession of several hundred formed, under the marshalship of Capt. Albert Wilford. At the tolling of the church bells, the procession moved to the Cemetery where the exercises consisted of singing, prayer, decorating the graves by returned soldiers, and hoisting the National flag at half-mast, to remain up till sunset.

It is but just that a few facts in connection with this matter be made known to the public. One would suppose that if friends and comrades desired to visit the sacred graves of fallen heroes, even on Sunday, they could do so in peace, and those who did not want to could also stay away in peace. But no sooner were the notices out than there was violent opposition to the whole movement, on the part of some who have more notoriety than wisdom or piety. One well known lawyer (?) here declared that he "would give $25 to decorate a rebel's grave, and would like to erect a monument to J. Wilkes Booth, as large as the depot wood-piles, *composed of the skulls of Union soldiers.*" Following in the wake of such expressions

17

was the action of the Common Council, who declined to be present on the occasion, and members of which, with others, took vigilant pains to circulate reports around the country that the chaplain and orator's name had been used without their consent, that the affair had been postponed, and endeavored to persuade the chaplain, singers and others to abandon the movement, as the leaders in the affair were only using them to give respectability to a training-day pow-wow. But notwithstanding all these obstacles, and the severe storm, a very large concourse gave, by their presence, their attestation of the occasion, while the ceremonies were very solemn, affecting and impressive.

After the ceremonies at the Cemetery, all the war-worn veterans repaired to their place of rendezvous and ventilated their pent-up feelings by voting unanimously the following, for publication:

Resolved, That our heart-felt thanks are due to all who have in any way assisted on this occasion, but that we can but express our deepest indignation at the course pursued by some members of the Common Council and others, in misrepresenting and embarrassing the movement, and that that body especially merit the severest censure for their conduct in this matter.

131

IN MEMORIAM.

BY COMRADE I. M. CRAVATH.

As I muse upon the visions
  That before my thoughts arise,
While I sit beside my tent-door
  In the twilight of the skies,
Darkness comes with solemn footsteps,
  Like the Patriarch at even,
And the angels build their camp-fires
  Round the battlements of heaven.

Gloomy shadows flit about me,
  And my soul is overcast;
But the forms of loved ones beckon
  From the threshold of the past,
And their deeds of kindness brighten
  All my thoughts with holy light,
Like the stars when sadly smiling
  Through the cloudy wings of night.

Once again my mother greets me—
  Her glad welcome in her eye—
And my father's hand is pressing
  Mine as in the days gone by,
And I hear a gentle sister
  Singing through the summer long,—
She has gone with them to heaven,
  But she left on earth the song.

Now within the dusky portal
  Come my comrades tried and true,
With the old, familiar footsteps,
  And the tones that once I knew;
Some with forms of stately beauty,—
  Some with eyes of heavenly blue,
And with voices like the angels'
  Song of midnight breaking through.

I recall the scene of conflict,
  With its "garments rolled in blood,"
And its line of daring heroes
  Where the front of battle stood,
And I see the dead and dying
  In my dreamings, as the years
Roll their mingling memories o'er me,
  Strangely blending smiles with tears.

APPENDIX.

The decoration ceremonies took place at the time appointed. The business places were all closed, and the exercises of the day participated in by business men generally. The Masonic and Odd Fellows' organizations attended and assisted the soldiers in decorating the graves. The procession, including teams, was very large.

The exercises at the grove, in the new Cemetery, were: Music by the Band; Prayer by Pres't Fairfield, of Hillsdale; Singing, by Misses Childs, Williams, and Messrs. Spencer, Smart, Power and Daniels—the music was very fine. Orations were delivered by Messrs. C. P. Brown and James Laird; after which, Pres't Fairfield made a speech some few minutes in length. Then followed the decoration of the graves of

J. C. Perkins, 15th Michigan Infantry.
Buel Chipman, 1st U. S Engineers.
Grant Durling, Hoffman's (Ohio) Battery.
Ira M. Bean, 59th Illinois Infantry.

After this, the procession moved to the old Cemetery, formed in hollow squares around the grave and monument of Capt. Samuel DeGolyer, while Chaplain Fairfield offered prayer. The monument of Capt. DeGolyer was tenderly and beautifully decorated. It was wrapped with the battle-flag presented him when he first entered the service, and carried us back over the eventful nine years to the time when we heard him thank the assembled people, and promise them that the flag should never be disgraced. He verified his word with his blood. His history is the history of the score of others that sleep around him. But we fear to linger upon a subject as touching as it is terrible. The graves decorated here were:

Capt. DeGolyer, Capt. Wm. H. Johnson, J. A. Hawkins, 1st Michigan Battery.
W. H. Thompson, Berdan's S. S.
J. G. Piper, 1st Michigan Infantry.
George O. Lawson, 4th Michigan Infantry.
George P. Hume, Kansas regiment.
W. A. Jones, New York regiment.
Wm. Davidson, James Thompson, Charles Wheeler, Justin McCoy, and W. H. Tolford, all of the 4th Michigan Infantry.

One of the saddest features of the day was the decoration of a spot of ground for Lieut. S. B. Preston, 4th Michigan.

Before the procession left the new Cemetery, it halted before and decorated the portion of empty ground set apart for a soldiers' monument.

DETROIT.

LIST OF SOLDIERS' GRAVES DECORATED, MAY, 1869.

Francis Anderson, Private, Co. D, 5th Infantry.
Wm. S. Whipple, Lieut. Colonel, 22d Infantry.
Cornelius Christie, Private, 18th Infantry.
Charles Mackenzie, Captain, 4th Cavalry.
—— Merrit, Captain, Co. H, 24th Infantry.
S. Jones Phillips, U. S. Navy.
James Moore, Private, 23d Ill. Infantry.
Henry Crane, Lieutenant, 3d Michigan Cavalry.
Thomas Ballard, Captain, 1st   "   "
Wellington Willets,   "   7th   "   "
Horace S. Sheldon, A. Q. M. 1st "   "
Henry W. Hall, Major, 24th Michigan Infantry.
Charles J. Snyder, Captain, 1st Cavalry.
William Noble, Lieutenant, 2d Infantry.
Dwight Stebbins, Volunteer Surgeon.
John D. Fairbanks, Major, 5th Infantry.
Wm. K. Coyl, Major, 9th Iowa Infantry.

Henry S. Hulbert, Captain.
Thomas Bloom, Drum Major, 1st Infantry.
Samuel Henry Eells, Assistant Surgeon, 12th Infantry.
J. D. Hall, Colonel, Illinois regiment.
Charles Skirrin, 4th Infantry.
Walter Stevenson, Captain, 5th Cavalry.
B. Thorpe, Lieutenant.
Louis Haidt, Lieutenant, 1st Battery.
Edward T. Owen, Lieutenant, 4th Cavalry.
E. Griffith Owen, A. Q. M., 1st Infantry.
John Mills, Private.
George Peabody, Private, Co. A, 51st Illinois Infantry.
S. R. Posey, Sergeant.
William Speed, Captain, 24th Infantry.
Frank Heig, Private, Co. D, 24th Infantry.
Irwin C. Darling, Private, 1st Wisconsin Cavalry.
Stephen B. Darling, Corporal, 6th Mich.   "
Henry Coville, Private, 9th Mich. Cavalry.
William Wright   "   9th Michigan Infantry.
——— Burrill, Lieutenant 24th   "   "
Ed. Wilson, Private, 24th   "   "
Chas. Crarey,   "   "   "   "
H. Adams, Serg't,   "   "   "
F. A. Buhl, Captain, 1st Cavalry.
Rob't Simson, Private 24th Infantry.
——— Phillips, Musician, 24th Infantry.
Wm. Hutchinson, Major,   "   ".
Henry Hutchinson, Captain, 8th   "
Thomas Williams, Brig. General, U. S. A.
——— Parsons, Private, 24th Infantry.
——— Broadhead, Colonel, 1st Cavalry.
Wm. Brevoort, Captain, 1st   "
Wm. Elliott,   "   "   "
Robert Elliott, Lieut. Col., 16th Infantry.
——— Nagle.
Toby Sherlock, Captain.
——— McLaughlin.
——— McCricket.
——— Johnston.
——— Roche.
J. Buckley.
M. Duran.
Seventy-three graves in Soldiers' Lot, names unknown.

OVID.

Timothy Brown, 14th Michigan Infantry.
Talman Beardsley, 10th Mich. Cavalry.
John Birely, 14th Ohio Infantry.
Evan Davis, 1st Michigan Cavalry.
Samuel Garrison, 14th Michigan Infantry.
George Fulkerson, 148th N. Y. Infantry.
Samuel Lane, 5th Michigan Infantry.
George Meddaugh, 4th Michigan Cavalry.
Anson L. Tyler, V. R. C.

List of Officers.

The following Officers were elected by the National Encampment assembled at Cincinnati, O., May 13, 1869 :

Comrade JOHN A. LOGAN, of Illinois, Commander-in-Chief.
" LUCIUS FAIRCHILD, of Wisconsin, Senior Vice Commander-in-Chief.
" JOSEPH R. HAWLEY, of Connecticut, Junior Vice Commander-in-Chief.
" S. P. WYLE MITCHELL, of Pennsylvania, Surgeon General.
" Rev. A. H. QUINT, of Massachusetts, Chaplain-General.

COUNCIL OF ADMINISTRATION.

Comrades J. F. MILLER, of California ; FRANK NOLEN, of Delaware ; R. M. HOUGH, of Illinois ; W. W. DUDLEY, of Indiana ; JOSEPH B. LEAK, of Iowa ; WM. BODEN, of Kentucky ; ANDREW W. DENISON, of Maryland ; J. WALDO DENNY, of Massachusetts ; OLIVER L. SPAULDING, of Michigan ; FRANK E. DAGGETT, of Minnesota ; G. HARRY STONE, of Missouri ; D. CARTER, of New Hampshire ; JAMES F. RUSLING, of New Jersey ; R. A. BACHIA, of New York ; GEO. L. BEALE, of Maine ; HARRY G. ARMSTRONG, of Ohio ; O. C. BOSBYSHELL, of Pennsylvania ; SAMUEL A. DUNCAN, of Washington ; JAMES SHAW, Jr., of Rhode Island ; R. KING SCOTT, of South Carolina ; G. G. MINOR, of Tennessee ; E. J. DAVIS, of Texas ; GEO. J. STANNARD, of Vermont ; CHARLES W. WICKERSHAM, of West Virginia ; GEO. P. GOODWIN, of Wisconsin.

OFFICERS APPOINTED BY THE COMMANDER-IN-CHIEF.

Comrade WILLIAM T. COLLINS, Adjutant-General.
" F. A. STARRING, Inspector-General.
" N. P. CHIPMAN, Judge-Advocate-General.
" TIMOTHY LUBEY, Quartermaster-General.
" HANSON E. WEAVER, Aide-de-Camp.

18

DEPARTMENT ROSTER.

Comrade WILLIAM HUMPHREY, of Lansing, Commander.
" GEO. M. BUCK, of Kalamazoo, Senior Vice Commander.
" JOHN K. GRAHAM, of Buchanan, Junior Vice Commander.
" II. II. DANIELS, of Lansing, Ass't Adj't General.
" A. O. SIMONS, of Lansing, Ass't Q. M. Gen.
" GEO. B. FLEMMING, of Charlotte, Inspector.
" A. B. RANNEY, of Three Rivers, Medical Director.
" L. O. SMITH, of Charlotte, Chaplain.

COUNCIL OF ADMINISTRATION.

Comrades S. II. Row, of Lansing; J. N. McFARLAN, of St. Johns; C. J. DICKERSON, of Hillsdale; WM. P. INNIS, of Grand Rapids; F. W. SWIFT, of Detroit.

AID-DE-CAMPS.

S. B. SMITH, Adrian; CHAS. II. HODSKIN, Battle Creek.

ROSTER OF POSTS.

Post No. 2, Battle Creek.

Commander, E. A. PRESTON.

S. V. C., WM. FLAGG.
J. V. C., V. WATTLES.
Adjutant, E. T. FREEMAN.
Quartermaster, J. F. RAYNES.

Surgeon, S. S. FRENCH.
Chaplain, JOB MOXOM.
Serg't Major, W. R. HORTON.
Q. M. Serg't, JAS. O. RILEY.

Post No. 4, St. Johns.

Commander, J. M. CARTER.

Post No. 5, Kalamazoo.

Commander, GEO. M. BUCK.

S. V. C., DARIUS ACKERLY.
J. V. C., ALFRED BROOKS.
Adj't, SIDNEY COOK.
Q. M., C. W. STONE.

Surg., AMOS D. ALLEN.
Chaplain, J. H. WELLS.
Serg't Major, J. J. DRAKE.
Q. M. Serg't, FRANK WHIPPLE.

Post No. 8, Duplain.

Commander, EZRA BROWN.

S. V. C., DENNIS BIRMINGHAM.

J. V. C., JOSEPH SEVER.

Adjutant, EDWARD T. WEALE.

Quartermaster, O. W. BIRMINGHAM.

Surgeon, JAMES G. WILCOX.

Chaplain, S. R. DEWSTOE.

Serg't Maj., J. M. BIRMINGHAM.

Q. M. Serg't, FRED. CARPENTER.

Woodbury Post, No. 12, Adrian.

Commander, J. II. FEE.

S. V. C., R. II. BAKER.

'J. V. C., J. D. HINCKLEY.

Adj., H. A. COLVIN.

Q. M., W. STEARNS.

Surg., R. T. MEAD.

Chaplain, W. II. KIMBALL.

Serg't Maj., G. P. ROBERTS.

Q. M. Serg't, C. W. DECKER.

Post No. 13, Ovid.

Commander, G. A. WINANS.

S. V. C., L. T. SOUTHWORTH.

J. V. C., DAVID ARMSTRONG.

Adj't, CHARLES COWAN.

Q. M., JOHN Q. PATTERSON.

Chaplain, J. C. DARRAGH.

Post No. 14, Hudson.

Commander, WILLIAM B. THOMPSON.

S. V. C., C. P. BROWN.

J. V. C., J. C. HANFORD.

Adj't, HARLOW McCARY.

Q. M., J. J. CARR.

Surgeon, L. C. FRENCH.

Chaplain, ED. M. HULBURD.

Serg't Major, ------ ------

Q. M. Serg't, M. L. PARKMAN.

Post No. 16, Sturgis.

Commander, EDMOND S. AMIDON.

S. V. C., NELSON I. PACKARD.

J. V. C., H. L. ANTHONY.

Adjt., M. D. KIRK.

Q. M., F. II. CHURCH.

Surgeon, ------ ------

Chaplain, ------ ------

Serg't Maj., ANDREW J. LAMB.

Q. M. Serg't, CHAS. E. LANDON.

140

Ed. Hurson Post, No. 18, Berrien Springs.

Commander, CHARLES E. HOWE.

S. V. C., HENRY G. POTTER.

J. V. C., JAMES H. DAVIDSON.

Adjt., FRANK N. DIX.

Q. M., DANIEL G. W. GANGLER.

Surgeon, JOSEPH C. WICOFF.

Chaplain, DAVID K. HUBBARD.

Serg't Maj., FRED. McOMBER.

Q. M. Serg't, JAMES N. PARKER.

Post No. 19, Ionia.

Commander, BENJAMIN R. COVERT.

S. V. C., JAMES V. MICKLE.

J. V. C., DAVID A. JEWELL.

Adj't, WILLIAM MILLIGAN.

Q. M., JOHN W. BANKS.

Surgeon, ——

Chaplain, HEMAN LOWE.

Serg't Maj., A. B. SIMMONS.

Q. M. Serg't, ISAAC VAN DORAN.

Post No. 21, Charlotte.

Commander, J. H. BOLTON.

S. V. C., GEO. FOREMAN.

J. V. C., PETER R. JOHNSON.

Adj't, L. E. DWINNELL.

Q. M., L. O. SMITH.

Chaplain, SOLOMON RICE.

Surgeon, ...

Serg't Major, ...

Q. M. Serg't, ...

Lumbard Post, No. 23, Hillsdale.

Commander, C. J. DICKERSON.

S. V. C., R. W. RICABY.

J. V. C., L. R. PENFIELD.

Adj't, L. E. GRIDLEY.

Q. M., WM. TAYLOR.

Surgeon, A. F. WHELAN.

Greene Post, No. 28, Lansing.

Commander, WILLIAM HUMPHREY.

S. V. C., E. H. PORTER.

J. V. C., S. H. ROW.

Adj't, J. W. KING.

Q. M., C. L. KNIGHT.

Surgeon, B. B. BAKER.

Chaplain, G. M. HASTY.

Serg't Maj., V. W. BRUCE.

Q. M. Serg't, F. M. HOWE

Turrell Post, No. 30, Lapeer.

Commander, MAYNARD BUTTS.

S. V. C., WM. M. SMITH.

J. V. C., STEWART GORTON.

Adj't, DERASTUS HOLMES.

Q. M., THOMAS MAIN.

Surgeon, ALFRED NASH.

Serg't Maj., PETER BASSETT.

Q. M. Serg't, DEXTER ADAMS.

Post No. 31, Edwardsburgh.

Commander, J. B. SWEETLAND.

S. V. C., WM. W. SWEETLAND.

J. V. C., J. W. ARGO.

Adj't, J. RANDOLPH.

Q. M., M. THOMAS.

Serg't Maj., C. MORGAN.

Q. M. Serg't, D. WATSON.

Post No. 32, Hastings.

Commander, NORMAN BAILEY.

S. V. C., TRAVERSE PHILLIPS.

J. V. C., L. A. CLARK.

Adj't, WM. MAYFORD.

Q. M., FRED. MAINE.

Surg., ISAAC W. BROOMAN.

Chaplain, WM. JONES.

Van Pelt Post, No. 34, Coldwater.

Commander, A. T. LAMPHERE.

S. V. C., MORTIMER MANSFIELD.

J. V. C., C. A. EDMONDS.

Adj't, L. A. DILLINGHAM.

Q. M., ANDREW GROSSE.

Surg., D. C. POWERS.

Chaplain, W. C. PORTER.

Serg't, Major, VAN DUNHAM.

Q. M. Sergt, D. B. PURINTON.

Post No. 39, Fairfield.

Commander, WILLIAM E. JORDAN.

S. V. C., RANSOM WALKER.

J. V. C., A. J. HOGGES.

Adj't, ALF. CHENEY.

Q. M., GEO. YOUNG.

Q. M. Serg't, S. F. MATSON.

Lewis Beagle Post, No. 42, Blissfield.

Commander, WILLIAM F. ROGERS.

S. V. C., JABEZ STEARNS.
J. V. C., L. D. BOONE.
Adj't, G. B. SMITH.

Q. M., MARTIN REHKLEW.
Serg't Maj., A. D. HAWES.
Q. M. Serg't, A. C. BOONE.

Slater Post, No. 43.

Commander, BENJAMIN E. BINNS.

S. V. C., W. I. HINES.
J. V. C., A. B. EVANS.
Adj't, WM. H. DAVIS.
Q. M., JNO. GRAHAM.

Surg., THEO. F. C. DODD.
Chaplain, F. W. HOLMES.
Serg't Major, G. H. WATSON.
Q. M. Serg't, JNO. S. CURTIS.

Prutzman Post, No. 44, Three Rivers.

Commander, R. R. PEALER.

S. V. C., W. H. H. WILCOX.
J. V. C., P. BINGHAM.
Adj't, JEFF. P. McKAY.
Q. M., A. W. SNYDER.

Surgeon, ISAAC KIMBALL.
Chaplain, JOHN S. DUNHAM.
Serg't Maj., B. WALTERS.
Q. M. Serg't, G. S. BAUM.

Eaton Post, No. 45, Otsego.

Commander, MILTON CHASE.

S. V. C., N. GILBERT.
J. V. C., SIDNEY ROUSE.
Adj't, H. F. GUEST.
Q. M., WM. A. ALLEN.

Surgeon, S. C. WEBSTER.
Chaplain, CHAS. D. PRENTISS.
Serg't Maj., WM. PALMER.
Q. M. Serg't, L. A. LEIGHTON.

Dick Richardson Post, No. 46, Detroit.

Commander, WM. A. THROOP.

S. V. C., A. M. EDWARDS.
J. V. C., W. R. DODSLEY.
Adj't, G. W. LaPOINTE.
Q. M., G. L. NADOLLECK.

Surg., D. V. BELL, JR.
Chaplain, F. W. SWIFT.
Serg't Maj., J. HARDY.
Q. M. Serg't, V. B. BELL.

Post No. 47, Tecumseh.

Commander, L. SAVIERS.

S. V. C., A. PELHAM.

J. V. C., CHAS. BIDWELL.

Adj't, A. W. SLAYTON.

Q. M., E. H. HOAG.

Chaplain, E. S. ORMSBY.

Serg't Major, _____ EMLAY.

Q. M., Serg't, H. B. STRICKLAND.

Wyker Post, No. 48, Owosso.

Commander, A. M. BEEBE.

S. V. C., E. GOULD.

J. V. C., H. H. CARSON.

Adj't, C. OSBURN.

Q. M., A. A. BARTLETT.

Surgeon, H. L. CHIPMAN.

Post No. 49, Grand Rapids.

Commander, W. P. INNES.

S. V. C., H. N. MOORE.

J. V. C., VAN E. YOUNG.

Adj't, J. D. DILLENBACK.

Q. M., F. J. FAIRBRASS.

Surgeon, C. W. EATON.

Chaplain, N. A. REED, Jr.

Serg't Maj., W. G. BECKWITH.

Q. M. Serg't, D. McNAUGHTON.

WILLIAM P. INNIS,

General Land and Business Agent,

GRAND RAPIDS, MICH.

Attends to the Purchase and Sale of

Farms, Wild Lands, Mills, Mill Sites, Town Lots,

CITY PROPERTY, BONDS & MORTGAGES.

Special Attention given to the Investigation of Tax Titles, Collection of Rents, Payment of Taxes, and Conveyancing.

OFFICE IN RATHBUN HOUSE BLOCK.

BRISBIN & CONELY,

(143 Washington Avenue,)

Lansing, - - - - Michigan,

DEALERS IN

Drugs, Chemicals, Patent Medicines,

GROCERIES, TRUSSES

— AND —

SHOULDER BRACES.

WHITE LEAD AND ZINCS BY THE CASE!

Raw and Boiled Linseed Oils, and Carbon Oil by the Barrel.

G. S. BRISBIN.   H. F. CONELY.

(Washington Avenue,)

Lansing, Michigan,

WHOLESALE & RETAIL DEALER

In all kinds of

CABINET WARE!

CHAIRS!

Willow Cabs, and Coffins!

THE LARGEST STOCK OF

FURNITURE

☞ ON HAND, ☜

Ever offered in Central Michigan!

PIERCE & PARMALEE,

Lansing, - - - - - - Michigan.

Sole Agents for the States of Michigan, Ohio and Indiana, for

Ruttan's Patent System of Ventilation!

Combined with

HAWLEY'S PATENT TUBULAR AIR WARMER.

RUTTAN's SYSTEM of Ventilating Buildings is the most SIMPLE
and PERFECT ever invented, consisting of openings in the Base-
Boards, communicating with the Chimney, and
furnishing in new buildings, without
extra expense, a

Perfect System of Ventilation,

Constantly Removing the Cold and Impure Atmosphere of Rooms.

HAWLEY'S AIR WARMER

Passes the Air to be used for Warming Rooms, through a
succession of Tubes similar to those used in Steam Boilers,
by which process the air is heated more rapidly,
and at a Less Expense of Fuel, than by any
other known. This combined system of
Heating and Ventilation,
is admirably adapted to

CHURCHES, SCHOOL-HOUSES,

AND ALL

Public Buildings and Private Dwellings,

*Supplying Pure, Warm Air in the Winter, and Fresh
Cool Air in Summer.*

Entire Satisfaction Guaranteed in all cases where the principles of this
System are [fully adopted, and a *saving of three-fourths of sickness*, and of
from one-third to one-half the expense of heating.

Ample References and Recommendations Given.

A. M. PIERCE, M. D.   **C. R. PARMALEE.**

BAKER & INGERSOLL,

Lansing, - - - Michigan,

MANUFACTURERS OF

AGRICULTURAL IMPLEMENTS!

Iron and Brass Castings,

CIRCULAR SAW MILLS,

STEAM ENGINES,

Ruttan's Warming and Ventilating Furnaces,

STONE'S PATENT SULKEY CULTIVATORS,

Grist Mill Furnishings, &c.

Also—Agents for and Dealers in

Massey's Combined Grain and Middling Feeder, Smutter and Separator,

STILWELL'S PATENT HEATER AND LIME CATCHER,

Being a thorough preventive against incrustation in Steam
Boilers and Pipes, insuring great saving in Fuel
and Durability of Boilers. Also,

Root's Sectional Wrought Iron Safety Boiler; also, C. &
J. Cooper's Steam Engines, Saw Mills, &c.; also,
Turbine Water Wheels, Belting, &c.

All at Lowest Cash Prices!

M. S. BAKER.   **ALEX. INGERSOLL.**

Corner of Capitol Ave. and Washtenaw St., west of Lansing House.

W. S. GEORGE & CO.,

DO ALL KINDS OF

BOOK, JOB, AND FANCY PRINTING;

BOOK BINDING & RULING.

———◆———

Make to Order,

BLANK BOOKS

For Business Men and Public Officers.

KEEP FOR SALE,

Law Blanks and Justice Dockets.

———

PUBLISH EVERY THURSDAY,

"THE LANSING STATE REPUBLICAN,"

A First Class Newspaper, and

The Best Advertising Medium in Central Michigan.

———

OFFICE:
Michigan Ave., nearly opposite State Offices. }   **LANSING, MICH.**

E. B. MILLAR & CO.,

(139 Washington Avenue,)

LANSING, - - - - - MICHIGAN.

Wholesale and Retail

DEALERS IN

GROCERIES!

CONSTANTLY IN STORE, A

Large Assortment of Goods

Belonging to the line, which we offer to the
Trade, or Consumers,

AT VERY LOW FIGURES!

Especially would we Invite Attention to our

LARGE STOCK OF

TEAS!

Embracing all the Different Varieties, at a very
Small Advance over Cost of Importation.

www.ingramcontent.com/pod-product-compliance
Lightning Source LLC
Chambersburg PA
CBHW020556270326
41927CB00006B/870